Field Theory in Child and Adolescent Psychoanalysis

Field Theory in Child and Adolescent Psychoanalysis looks at the intersection of two types of psychoanalysis that challenge the classic model: child analysis, and field theory.

Children impose a faster pace on the analysis and a much less stable structure than adults, whilst psychoanalytic field theory looks at the patient-analyst relationship in a much wider context than is typical. By combining these two approaches, this book advocates the use of a set of tools and techniques that allow the psychoanalyst to understand and react much faster than normal and to be better prepared for unexpected developments. This book shows the reader how to navigate smoothly and steadily through passages of tense analytical situations, which might otherwise feel like being trapped in a maze with no obvious way out.

Bion's writings allowed the improvement of new techniques or instruments for exploring the psychoanalytical process. Discussion about technique is a hugely important and necessary step for improving the evidence base of psychoanalytic psychotherapy. This book also seeks to improve the research in therapeutic effectiveness and unexpected relations between body and mind, emotions and dreams. By doing so, Elena Molinari contributes to expanding the perspectives that child and adolescent psychoanalysts have had in exploring primitive functioning of the mind.

With specific emphasis on working with difficult situations and patients, *Field Theory in Child and Adolescent Psychoanalysis* is a highly practical book that will appeal greatly to child psychoanalysts and psychoanalytic psychotherapists as well as psychologists, paediatricians and advanced students studying across these fields.

Elena Molinari is a psychoanalyst of the Italian Psychoanalytic Society and an IPA member. She began her professional life working as a paediatrician. Since 2000, she has worked as a private analyst with adults and children. Since 2004, she has been teaching 'Child Neuropsychiatry' for the postgraduate course in art therapy at the Academy of Fine Arts of Brera, Milan. Since 2013, she has been a Section Editor of the SPI journal *Rivista di Psicoanalisi*.

Psychoanalytic Field Theory Book Series

The Routledge Psychoanalytic Field Theory Book Series was initiated in 2015 as a new subseries of the Psychoanalytic Inquiry Book Series. The series publishes books on subjects relevant to the continuing development of psychoanalytic field theory. The emphasis of this series is on contemporary work that includes a vision of the future for psychoanalytic field theory.

Since the middle of the twentieth century, forms of psychoanalytic field theory emerged in different geographic parts of the world with different objectives, heuristic principles and clinical techniques. Taken together, they form a family of psychoanalytic perspectives that employs a concept of a bi-personal psychoanalytic field. The Psychoanalytic Field Theory Book Series seeks to represent this pluralism in its publications. Books on field theory in all its diverse forms are of interest in this series. Both theoretical works and discussions of clinical technique will be published in this series.

The series editors are especially interested in selecting manuscripts which actively promote the understanding and further expansion of psychoanalytic field theory. Part of the mission of the series is to foster communication amongst psychoanalysts working in different models, in different languages and in different parts of the world.

Titles in this series:

Vol. 1 Contemporary Psychoanalytic Field Theory: Stories, Dreams, and Metaphor
S. Montana Katz

Vol. 2 Advances in Contemporary Psychoanalytic Field Theory: Concept and Future Development
Edited by S. Montana Katz, Roosevelt Cassorla & Giuseppe Civitarese

Vol. 3 Field Theory in Child and Adolescent Psychoanalysis: Understanding and Reacting to Unexpected Developments
Elena Molinari

Field Theory in Child and Adolescent Psychoanalysis

Understanding and Reacting to Unexpected Developments

Elena Molinari

LONDON AND NEW YORK

First published 2017
by Routledge
2 Park Square, Milton Park, Abingdon, Oxon OX14 4RN

and by Routledge
711 Third Avenue, New York, NY 10017

Routledge is an imprint of the Taylor & Francis Group, an informa business

© 2017 Elena Molinari

The right of Elena Molinari to be identified as author of this work has been asserted by her in accordance with sections 77 and 78 of the Copyright, Designs and Patents Act 1988.

All rights reserved. No part of this book may be reprinted or reproduced or utilised in any form or by any electronic, mechanical, or other means, now known or hereafter invented, including photocopying and recording, or in any information storage or retrieval system, without permission in writing from the publishers.

Trademark notice: Product or corporate names may be trademarks or registered trademarks, and are used only for identification and explanation without intent to infringe.

British Library Cataloguing-in-Publication Data
A catalogue record for this book is available from the British Library

Library of Congress Cataloging-in-Publication Data
Names: Molinari, Elena, 1960– author.
Title: Field theory in child and adolescent psychoanalysis : understanding and reacting to unexpected developments / Elena Molinari.
Description: Abingdon, Oxon ; New York, NY : Routledge, 2017. | Includes bibliographical references and index.
Identifiers: LCCN 2016048448 | ISBN 9781138686724 (hbk : alk. paper) | ISBN 9781138686731 (pbk. : alk. paper) | ISBN 9781315542584 (ebk)
Subjects: | MESH: Psychoanalytic Therapy—methods | Psychology, Child | Psychology, Adolescent | Psychoanalytic Theory | Professional-Patient Relations
Classification: LCC RJ504 | NLM WS 350.5 | DDC 618.92/8917—dc23
LC record available at https://lccn.loc.gov/2016048448

ISBN: 978-1-138-68672-4 (hbk)
ISBN: 978-1-138-68673-1 (pbk)
ISBN: 978-1-315-54258-4 (ebk)

Typeset in Times New Roman
by Apex CoVantage, LLC

To Paolo, and Cecilia, Beatrice, Roberto

Contents

	List of figures	viii
	Acknowledgements	ix
1	From one room to the other: a story of contamination – the relationship between child and adult analysis	1
2	Luigi and the cinématographe, the first motion-picture camera	23
3	An analyst learns to play: from crumpled-up paper to origami	36
4	A 'quantum' of truth in a field of lies: the investigation of emotional truth in a child analysis	54
5	The anteroom: a camera obscura for grasping aspects that are invisible in the classical setting	74
6	The use of child drawings to explore the dual ↔ group analytic field in child analysis	88
7	Sunday cartoons and very young patients	110
8	Action across emptiness	129
	Bibliography	146
	Index	156

Figures

1.1	Awareness of movement	12
1.2	The family of Giuseppe	17
1.3	Giuseppe in hibernation like an insect	17
2.1	First drawing on a squared paper	28
2.2	Furniture and alarm systems in Luigi's room	29
2.3	'Grolla' or crafted cup	31
2.4	House inside a castle	32
4.1	Map of α elements incapable to evolve	60
4.2	Map of transformation of a β element into an α one	69
5.1	Under Alice's shoes	79
6.1	Room of Elisa's parents	95
6.2	Parents at work	97
6.3	Wedding of parents	100
6.4	Trip to the analyst's room	103
6.5	Susan Hiller, Dream Mapping, Notebook, 1974	107
6.6	Susan Hiller, Dream Mapping, Collective Work, 1974	108
7.1	Sunday cartoon: field's expansion	114
7.2	Daily strip: persecutory object	117
7.3	Sunday cartoon: analyst's unavailability	118
7.4	Sunday cartoon: an unexpected event	125
8.1	Squiggle with objects	139
8.2	Pole voltage and electric wire	141
8.3	Orange juice extractor	142
8.4	The connected meter	143
8.5	Meter with free-floating strings	144

Acknowledgements

Every effort has been made to contact the copyright holders for their permission to reprint selections of this book. The publishers would be grateful to hear from any copyright holder who is not here acknowledged, and we will undertake to rectify any errors or omissions in future editions of this book.

Chapter 1 first published as Molinari, E. (2011), From one room to the other: a story of contamination. The relationship between child and adult analysis, *International Journal of Psychoanalysis*, vol. 92; pp. 791–810. Reprinted by permission of John Wiley & Sons, Inc.

Excerpt in Chapter 1 from 'Lappin and Lappinova' from A HAUNTED HOUSE AND OTHER SHORT STORIES by Virginia Woolf. Copyright 1944 by Houghton Mifflin Harcourt Publishing Company. Copyright © renewed 1972 by Houghton Mifflin Harcourt Publishing Company. Reprinted by permission of Houghton Mifflin Harcourt Publishing Company. All rights reserved.

Figure 1.1 first featured in *Il movimento disegna*. Di Renzo, M., Nastasi, I. E. (1989) Roma, Armando. Reprinted with the kind permission of Armando Editore.

Excerpt from *The Daydreamer* by Ian McEwan. Copyright © 1995 Ian McEwan. Published by Jonathan Cape. Reprinted by permission of The Random House Group Limited and Doubleday Canada, a division of Penguin Random House Canada Limited.

Chapter 2 first published as Molinari, E. (2004), Luigi e la machinna del cinema, *Quarderni di psicoterapia infantile*, vol. 49; pp. 231–244. Reprinted by permission of Edizioni Borla.

The epigraph featured at the start of Chapter 2 is taken from *I racconti* by G. Tomasi di Lampedusa, Feltrinelli, Milano, 1961. Reprinted by permission of Giangiacomo Feltrinelli Editore.

Chapter 3 first published as Molinari, E. (2011), From crumpled-up paper to origami: an analyst learns to play, *The Psychoanalytic Quarterly*, vol. 80; pp. 857–878. Reprinted by permission of John Wiley & Sons, Inc.

The epigraph featured at the start of Chapter 3 is taken from *La compagnia dei celestini* by S. Benni, Feltrinelli, Milano, 1992. Reprinted with permission of Giangiacomo Feltrinelli Editore.

Chapter 4 first published as Molinari, E. (2011), A 'quantum' of truth in a field of lies: the investigation of emotional truth in a child analysis, *International Journal of Psychoanalysis*, vol. 92; pp. 1483–1500. Reprinted by permission of John Wiley & Sons, Inc.

The *Calvin and Hobbes* cartoons featured in Chapter 4 are reprinted with the kind permission of Universal Uclick. CALVIN AND HOBBES © 1993 Watterson. Reprinted with permission of UNIVERSAL UCLICK. All rights reserved. CALVIN AND HOBBES © 1986 Watterson. Reprinted with permission of UNIVERSAL UCLICK. All rights reserved. CALVIN AND HOBBES © 1992 Watterson. Reprinted with permission of UNIVERSAL UCLICK. All rights reserved.

Chapter 5 first published as Molinari, E. (2013), The anteroom: a camera obscura for grasping aspects that are invisible in the classical setting, *The Psychoanalytic Quarterly*, vol. 82; pp. 811–827. Reprinted by permission of John Wiley & Sons, Inc.

Chapter 6 first published as Molinari, E. (2013), The use of drawings to explore dual ↔ group analytical field in child analysis, *International Journal of Psychoanalysis*, vol. 94; pp. 293–312. Reprinted by permission of John Wiley & Sons, Inc.

Figure 6.5 'Susan Hiller, Dream Mapping, Notebook, 1974' and Figure 6.6 'Susan Hiller, Dream Mapping, Collective Work, 1974' (also used for the cover of this book) are featured with the kind permission of Susan Hiller.

Epigraph featured at the start of Chapter 7 is taken from *Calvin and Hobbes: Sunday Pages 1985–1995* © 2001 Bill Watterson (Andrews McMeel Publishing). Reprinted with kind permission.

Chapter 8 first published as Molinari, E. (2014), Action across emptiness, *Journal of Child Psychotherapy*, 40:3; pp. 239–253. Reprinted by permission of Taylor & Francis, LLC.

Chapter 1

From one room to the other

A story of contamination – the relationship between child and adult analysis

> The room had its passions and rages and envies and sorrows coming over it and clouding it, like a human being.
>
> Virginia Woolf[1]

The door to my office opens onto a small waiting room: to the left an ordinary glass door leads to the consulting room for adult patients; to the right a sliding door with stained-glass windows gives way to the consulting room for children. On countless occasions, passing from one room to the other over the course of a day's work, I would allow the reflection of the coloured glass to appear and disappear on the wall without thinking too deeply about which features were common to the work that took place in these two separate spaces and which were particular to each.

For a long time, I was satisfied with the idea that in both rooms I was attempting to practise psychoanalysis and that the difference in what took place in the two rooms was based on a divergence in technique and language. One day, however, as I opened the coloured door leading to the children's room, designed in the style of a Mondrian painting, I realized that my love of painting and psychoanalysis met at a point within myself. It seemed to me as if in one room there was a type of psychoanalysis which resembled literature and in the other a type of psychoanalysis which resembled visual art. Upon further reflection, I was surprised to discover that, within the sphere of the theoretical model that underpinned my analytical practice, certain events that had taken place in the children's room had silently modified the implicit theoretical model which I used in my work with adults. This chapter is an attempt to define the particular features of child analysis and to share my experience of the transformative role which the practice of child analysis can have on one's work with adults.

A historically difficult relationship

The aim of psychoanalysis is not to create an artistic product but is in fact the process through which one carries out analytic work; this *"is not unlike the complex, tormented, and exhilarating gestation of a work of art"*.[2] The idea that child analysis is closer to painting and adult analysis to literature came to me through reading Virginia Woolf's diaries and her correspondence with her sister, Vanessa Bell. These two women competed with each other using two different forms of expression – literature and painting – and engaged in an intense dialogue, provoking and inspiring a reciprocal investigation of each other. I cite here a few extracts from this correspondence to illustrate how the relationship between child and adult analysis has historically played out. *"Surely you must see the infinite superiority of the language to the paint?"* wrote Virginia Woolf to her nephew in 1928.[3] The author here captures the sense of privilege which the word has enjoyed in Western culture: a tradition of thought which has treated first *logos* and then the word as the privileged vehicle for communication.

Scant interest has typically been shown for images when they are in a direct relationship with a text, serving the function of illustrating it. They are merely regarded as useful as an aid to comprehension and as a way of making the words more appetizing. The relationship between word and image became a source of bitter conflict between the two sisters when Vanessa attempted to illustrate some of Virginia's writings in a way that broke with the traditional understanding of illustration. She not only did not illustrate the contents but also ended up decorating the page in such a way as to obscure some of the written text. This episode may be compared, albeit with some caution, to the first steps of child psychoanalysis.

Freud's position rested on the idea that child analysis could not satisfy what was then deemed indispensable for performing analytical therapy: a sufficiently developed ego and the presence of a repressed trauma which could be cured by being re-experienced in the transference of neurosis. It is for this reason that Freud regarded child analysis as an application of the principles of psychoanalysis to pedagogy, a useful instrument for testing the hypotheses about child development that he formulated by induction through his adult patients' memories.[4] By contrast, Melanie Klein[5] maintained the existence of a primitive ego capable of producing phantasies within the first months of life, thus detaching the unconscious phantasy from the mechanism of repression which made such phantasy possible only later, at the twilight of the Oedipus complex. With Susan Isaacs's contribution,[6] the unconscious phantasy assumed in those years an ever more central position in the analytic process, eventually coinciding with the unconscious activity present from birth. This progressive theorization of a highly primitive unconscious phantasy entailed overthrowing the historical paradigm of reconstruction and paved the way for the development of the idea that the unconscious phantasy, encouraged by the encounter with the analyst, is what gives life to any gesture or narrative in the consulting room. Unconscious phantasies, like dreams and oneiric thought more generally, make use of a primarily iconic code for which both Melanie Klein and Vanessa Bell claimed an autonomous communicative power. At a conference at Leighton Park School, Vanessa Bell articulated the foundational principle of her aesthetic by affirming that, while novelists claim to depict reality, they do not really see it but observe it by describing its details. On the contrary, it is the painters who succeed in depicting reality, since their main concern is the study of colour in relation to the form of objects and the space surrounding them.[7]

From the same perspective, one can argue that child psychoanalysis has not turned out to be, as Freud thought, an application of adult analysis but the catalyst for Bion's epistemological revolution. Indeed, in spite of never having worked with children, Bion integrated into his thought the insights yielded by child analysis into the origins of thinking and the earliest forms of mental activity, building upon these premises a theory different from the one based on the instinctual model.[8] Now that the debate, with its roots in these theoretical differences, has become amicable in nature, allowing for a dialogue between the pulsional model and that of the development of thinking, I would like to show how the two arts – of child and adult psychoanalysis – continue to influence and stimulate each other in clinical work.

Following Bion, some authors maintain that there is no difference in the development of oneiric thought in waking life taking place during analytic sessions. To use Bionian terms, the α function – that is, the mental function that consents to the transformation of the β elements (proto-emotions and proto-sensations) into visual pictograms – works in the same way, irrespective of whether an analyst uses actual play or the account of play. These authors thus maintain that it is possible and useful for the analyst to translate a session from the language of children into that of adults. This is tantamount to demonstrating that the same scene can be described and illustrated using two different languages without bringing about substantial differences in the analytic process. In keeping with this line of thought, since the two practices are mutually reinforcing, child analysis can refine the analyst's sensitivity to forms of expression other than words. While sharing these ideas, the debate between Vanessa Bell and Virginia Woolf has led me to ask the following question: although I may make use of the same theoretical model, do I really perform similar mental operations in the children's and adults' consulting rooms?

In the children's consulting room

Reflecting on my experience, I feel I am a different psychoanalyst in the two consulting rooms in several respects. A first way of describing this sensation is to say that, when I work with children, I think less. When I am with children, I immerse myself in practical activities and in a series of actions which constitute play in such a way as to carry me further away from reflective thought than is the case in my adult practice. In a sense, child analysis is an experience in which Bion's recommendation that the psychoanalyst "*abandons memory and desire (in order to be optimally intuitive and receptive to his own unconscious vis-a-vis the analysand)*"[9] comes naturally. The shift away from theory, induced by action, produces a distance from reflective thought and from what can be experienced as cluttering the mind.

A second difference becomes apparent when writing notes after a session. One finds oneself organizing the content of a session of adult or child analysis in a logical and systematic way that does not reflect the reality. One tends to organize the analytical interaction in such a way as to omit what one has not understood or what one's consciousness has failed to translate into words. When writing up notes on a session of child analysis, I have a far greater sense of the presence of inexpressible fragments, whether in terms of the sequence of the play or in the meaning of the narrative. Accompanying this is the sensation of having incorporated many images into a process which comes close to a kind of slow assimilation, until I feel as though the images have become my own. I have suggested that the faster rhythm of one's interaction with children is in a way counterbalanced by the slower rhythm of one's elaboration. The child induces the analyst to take longer over the rhythmic and sensory structure of the interaction: the mind requires more time to move from this type of interaction to symbolization, however we wish to understand it. The resulting idea is that of a loss of control over the progress of symbolic transformation, an idea that is masked by a vague sense of unease.

When working with children, I am inclined to represent emotions in a more figurative and pictorial form, with the result that I risk ending up in a silent internal space where the idea of a cure comes closer to a sense of moving together towards the production of symbolic forms.

The analytic game

The suspension of action has been one of the fundamentals of the analytic method so that even in child analysis the analyst is limited to accompanying or interpreting the child's games with words. Kleinian analysts in particular have theorized about the importance of the analyst's remaining outside the play in order to understand its meaning.[10] Whereas for these analysts the aesthetic sphere of playing – by contrast with the rational sphere – was considered to be of little use for knowing and understanding things in an analytical way, for Winnicott, playing became not only a means to represent the unconscious but also a vehicle for conveying different meanings. Playing became for Winnicott a category for what was possible, placing both the psychoanalyst and the child in the moment at which things begin to take shape. Almost like a kind of arising *logos*, during the generative moment, playing manages to take the analytic couple towards a form of representation similar to that of Chinese poetry. Here, most of the ideographical roots preserve in themselves a verbal idea of action, and the thing, which remains indistinct from action, includes its movement in a dynamic framework. Moreover, all subjects of analysis, initially performing actions, engage in a dialogue with what concerns them, until these actions become significant, receiving meaning not from an external attribution but from the same conscious and unconscious action that generates them.

Taking this idea to its extreme conclusion, Winnicott overturns the system of references by making playing, previously just an instrument in the psychoanalytic process, the foundational element of analysis. Indeed, he goes so far as to define the psychoanalytic process as "*a highly specialized form of playing in the service of communication with oneself and others*".[11]

Having expanded our theoretical horizons, Winnicott is also the catalyst for important shifts in the theory of technique. When describing his way of interacting with children through squiggles, Winnicott[12] comes across as an analyst capable of actively participating in the creation of graphic representations and, at the same time, willing actively to reveal something about himself in relation to the process as it occurs.

After Winnicott, it was above all the object-relations analysts who took up some of the ideas just discussed and theorized about the need for the child analyst to be entirely immersed in the metaphor of play so as to actively participate in the creation of possible meanings. Many analysts today share the notion that playing is a therapeutic process in itself and not a process in the activation of other therapeutic processes.[13] Moreover, the interpersonal relationship, with its many moments of real contact and separation, finds in Winnicott's account of playing a physical representation of the ruptures and healing capacities that a child experiences in relation to the mother. These aspects of playing have been greatly enriched by observing the role of the bonding of mother and child in the development of the capacity to work through emotions and develop healthy relationships.[14]

As an instrument for the development of various possible stories, playing is in the end an essential instrument for analysts who privilege as the goal of analysis the expansion of the bi-personal field and the development of the mental container of both members of the analytic couple.[15] One technical implication of the theoretical developments briefly summarized earlier is that verbal interpretation has become less important for child analysis than for adult analysis. At times, this kind of interpretation can even risk becoming harmful if it interrupts the natural process by which the child comes to make the distinction between phantasy and reality through the expansion of the phantasy itself.[16] I will now attempt to answer the question with which I began: is there a difference between the physical playing which is practised in the child's consulting room and the primarily verbal one which characterizes analytical work with adults?

The body and playing in relation to *reverie*

My hypothesis about how children's play could produce specific processes is derived from Marion Milner's reflection on the creative process in drawing. Milner believes that, in order to draw, two mental functions are necessary: a reflective function and the capacity to abandon oneself to the unconscious. If one pays excessive attention to one's original intentions, then the drawing will turn out to be rigid and ugly; on the other hand, if one becomes hostage to the lines which appear casually on the page, then the drawing will come closer to resembling a daydream. For this reason, Milner concludes, it is necessary for there to be a dialogue between action and thought in drawing, and it is the encounter between unconscious thought and action which gives rise to the development of daydreaming.[17]

Following in her footsteps, I also believe that in analysis, in whatever form it is practised, dreaming and having ideas become entwined so as to give life to a creative and transformative process. I agree with Ferro and Basile when they claim that *"even with adolescents and adults, we can learn to interpret as if we were 'playing' or 'drawing'; that is as if we were using words in a drawing that continually undergoes change, enrichment, and variation in color"*.[18] However, *"as if"* implies that drawing and using words as if they were a game or a drawing nevertheless remain two distinct operations, produced through different mental processes. Whereas in the adult consulting room it is the body's immobility that is fundamental to the dreaming function of the mind, in the child's consulting room, the opposite takes place, and thus it is the action that generates the reverie. In the child's consulting room, the encounter with the action of playing yields thought capable of playing with itself, thought which, like a kind of arising *logos*, mixes unconscious and reflective thought in a peculiar way.

When I am working with children, daydreams emerge very quickly through playing, and I know that, just as if I were painting, I will be unable for some time to reflect on the process with a clear frame of mind. Both in painting and in playing, it is action that guides thought, and reflection is only possible when one feels that the process has reached a certain level of development. Only then is it possible to take a step back, making observations and reflecting from a distance.

The mental process which I am attempting to describe, and which is located specifically in thought born from action and not from its suspension, is also present in the very language which children use. When, for example, a child takes an object and says, 'Let's say this was a gun', he does not mean 'Let's pretend that this object really is a gun'. This 'let's say' language forcibly leads the therapist towards a symbolic register which is different from the one implied by the verbs 'to imagine' or 'to think'. When a child says, 'Let's say', he means that we should use our bodies and not look at the shape of the object in question through the cognitive register which allows us to recognize it for what it is. Our hands will have to shape a new object through the gestures of playing, and our eyes will see it through a register of imagination which is different from the one belonging to the symbolic code of language. Besides, when he says, 'Let's pretend this was . . .', the child also makes it possible for the analyst to reach him in a transitional space, suddenly transported by this incorrect use of the past tense to a different time – a time which could really have to do with the past, or perhaps more likely, with the future of creativity.

A further aspect that contributes to creating in child analysis a different mode of thought from adult analysis, one that resembles that of painting, has to do with the use of toys. Even if toys can be utilized as if they were characters in a story, often as soon as a child begins to play, he becomes at one with the objects he uses. The therapist too soon is placed in a kind of fusional relationship with these objects, similar to the one painters adopt in order to be able to draw. This change of perspective, which Milner calls *"concentration of the body"*, in turn produces a distraction from the symbolic meaning while increasing attention towards forms. Thus, when I play with a child, I often find myself involuntarily being more receptive not only to the forms of objects but also to those shapes which the child creates in the room by running around, picking up and throwing down many objects in fast succession, and repeating the same action in a rhythmic way. These moving forms capture my attention and produce a variation in the way of perceiving emotions. Rather than understanding through countertransference, which is a sensation that is born from within, I feel through a kind of involvement which revolves around seeing and which entails avoiding tracing clear boundaries between oneself and the other or between oneself and objects – a feeling similar to that of being moved by a painting. At times, I even feel anxious about being captured by this way of feeling, with the result that my capacity to think will remain subjugated by it. On other occasions, however, the sense of being exempted from reflective thought grants me a greater freedom of invention or creativity than exists with adults. For the two reasons just described – that is, the mediation of the body which playing necessarily entails and the specificity of the reverie which the body in action produces – I do not carry out identical mental operations in the children's and adults' consulting rooms, in spite of making use of the same theoretical model.

Child analysis is thus shown to result from a different creative process from that of adult analysis, one which is closer to that of figurative art.

In the penultimate session before the summer holidays, Luca, a seven-year-old boy in analysis three times a week, comes into the consulting room holding a toy he had just bought in a shop near my office. It was a target virtually identical to mine. He wants me to hang it directly on top of mine and starts throwing adhesive balls against it.

I tell him, 'In this way, our two games are close to each other; this summer, however, they will be far apart, one in your room and one here in mine. But when we play alone, we will remember that we have played together in the past and that we can do it again'.

Luca ignores me and, understanding the meaning of his indifference, I propose another interpretation, which also recalls the difficulty of our separation and the possibility of our overcoming it by thinking about each other. Luca, irritated, silences me: 'Stop it. Don't speak! You're spoiling the game!'

Soon after, Luca goes into the bathroom next to the consulting room and turns off the light so as to create an environment which, in his fantasy, is a dark cave. In the game, the bathroom has become a providential shelter from a storm. At first, Luca is very agitated; his fear of and anger at what he cannot see, and his sense of impotence against the forces of nature, are emotions that express themselves through his body.

Keeping very close to this motor-sensorial register, I remark, 'You know, everything is black for me, too, and my heart is beating really fast'.

In another moment, pretending to follow the flight and cry of some bats, I say, 'We are agitated just like bats when they are afraid'.

Out of this physical agitation, Luca gradually develops the hope of possible closeness and starts pretending we are husband and wife, living in extreme poverty. Luca asks me not to move in order to induce in my body a greater sense of calm; he tells me to stay in the cave where there is no danger, while he goes out, initially without an apparent purpose, then bringing firewood, food and finally a furry mouse on successive trips. After bringing these provisions, and still in semi-darkness, we can cook and eat together.

After the session, I realize that what I had mistaken for indifference was in fact a defence against a too intense emotion, inadequately symbolized and difficult to share. I also understand why he reacted with such unhappiness and irritation to my words: not only did they fail to take into account the extent of his capacity to comprehend and digest the painful emotions associated with our separation but also words of any kind were far from being what he needed in that moment. As Luca himself indicated, words risked spoiling the game, through which his and my mind could offer a physical expression of sensations such as deprivation, coldness, hunger and loneliness resulting from a forced separation. A transformation had been produced not through my verbal interpretation but through my playing with Luca, sharing his feelings and myself accepting the momentary separation. After having placed me out of harm's way, in the game but also in his own mind, Luca experiences leaving and coming back several times from our shared house, learning to take control of the next long separation and finding in himself the ability to procure firewood, food and even a small animal (which he told me was a canal rat), allowing him to let out his aggression in a non-destructive way. Through playing, Luca finds a very effective representation of his emotive turbulence (the storm) and the need for a container within which the α function could generate a series of images capable of giving meaning to previously unthinkable emotions.

What must be emphasized is the way in which the child and I created the play. In the bathroom, Luca feels the same anxiety of a painter in front of a blank canvas or page: an anxiety significant because of the distance between oneself and the object one has invested with emotions, an anxiety which finds a first form of containment in the dark of the uterine container. Luca's body is initially filled with emotions that have neither form nor name. It is not easy to describe with words the uncertain way in which meaning takes shape from this initial chaos, and then through successive attempts, often begun and then immediately abandoned. At times, it is as if the child had an inkling of an overabundance of pseudo-aesthetic shapes which take him away from a true working through, or, on the contrary, of forms which are emotionally too frightening and which shape his production of moving images. What, however, becomes clear while we share in the experience of the play is that the child develops a perceptive capacity through playing, from which it is possible to hypothesize that the game is not only a form of representation but also a tool for the creation of parts of the self. Moreover, the hypothesis that the verbal form may not have been suitable for encouraging this process has enabled me to become involved in the creation of an action capable of bringing about the first seed of a phantasy contained within the target-hitting game.

This game was indeed the start of a process through which Luca had come to make his first symbolic attempt emotionally to experience our separation by watching how the balls stuck to the target before being suddenly ripped off. The development of this early attempt to think could take place only by allowing the child to continue the process through a figurative representation. In the absence of this awareness in the earlier example, I could have insisted on the intolerance of Luca towards the separation, thus removing his creative capacity to bring together through action his reflective capacity with the unconscious phantasies aroused in him from the imminent separation.

Elements of contamination between the two rooms

Beyond the specificity of the relationship and language which makes every encounter between patient and analyst unique, there are certain aspects which differentiate my mental functioning when working with children and with adults. Some of these aspects which, broadly speaking, have to do with an aesthetic sensibility (that is, more with form than with content), are born from within the practice of child analysis. Occasionally, I become more aware of what I have learnt from children by working with adult patients and consequently have also been able to use this knowledge with them.

Using sensory faculties to begin to represent what one is not yet able to understand fully

I will now draw on an example taken from the development of graphic expressive capacities in the representation of the body. From my personal experience in this area, four-year-old children are unable to draw the body in motion. A more detailed investigation[19] has instead revealed that children are capable of expressing the idea of motion in original and unexpected ways, using vague bodily sensations generated by movement (see Figure 1.1). The strategy that makes the child capable of representing movement in an effective way originates not in a capacity to transfer

Figure 1.1 Awareness of movement

what he sees on to the page but in allowing himself to be immersed into the sensorial memory of the experience. When drawing, the child does not copy a mental image but starts from the sensations which the body experiences through action or in relation with an object. This graphic example allows us to appreciate the importance of the sensorial and perceptive faculties for the initial structuring of representations, but, above all, it constitutes an example of the way in which the child's capacity for thought can evolve, integrating sensations with images more than we can imagine through an awareness of the development of figurative representation.

This kind of experience has indeed also changed my mental approach with adults (in particular with those with a deficiency of the α function), with whom I have become better able to promote representations through the use of sensation images, before being able to use images to evoke emotions. What follows is a clinical example taken from my work with an adult patient.

After the birth of his son, Mr F's relational difficulties culminated in episodes of child abuse and in a revival of homosexual desires, resulting in his separating from his wife. Mr F had unexpectedly lost his own father at a young age and had then spent the rest of his childhood at boarding school, where he experienced physical and psychological violence.

Being already aware that his mother was having an affair with another man, he experienced his estrangement as a function of his mother's desire to get rid of him.

After several years in analysis four times a week, Mr F dreams that he is at home in his bedroom and is being caressed and enveloped from behind by the loving arms of a man. At first, the dream is very pleasant, but then his partner's arms begin to tighten around him, and he feels a highly distressing sense of suffocation. He wriggles away and, still within the dream, he wakes up with much effort and, turning the light on, sees a black shadow which he persistently tries to grab. His anxiety interrupts his sleep and the dream breaks off, but – now awake – he sees (in the form of a hallucination) the shadow from the dream in his own bedroom. The confusion of the boundary between the realities of dream and waking life is so anxiety provoking that in the dead of night he leaves his house and goes to his mother's. Commenting on his dream, Mr F highlights how the most unpleasant feeling was initially that of suffocation but then also the sensation that his body was too heavy to be able to keep up with the shadow projected onto the wall. 'I felt as though my body were heavy and rigid, incapable of moving, as if a mysterious force were pinning me down on the bed . . . I couldn't tell if I was dead or alive!'

Without communicating it to Mr F, it occurs to me that in the dream he regards his way of establishing contact through a kind of sexuality which suffocates his rational and emotional faculties as death-inducing. Through the feeling of being pleasantly held from behind, Mr F then recovers the memory of a photograph of himself as a child and his father, taken just as they were shooting at a target at a funfair. As the only photo of his father smiling and tightly hugging him, it allows Mr F to begin to understand how his sexual desire could have something to do with a desire more intimate and dangerous than his relationship with his father, a relationship which had been violently interrupted as if by gunshot.

Thinking about how children can conquer the capacity to represent new faculties through bodily sensations, I decide to speak to Mr F about the tension which he seemed to have experienced in the dream in order to reach and understand (through touch) the shadow on the wall and about the way he confronted the distance from his mother.

While saying this, I think about how in the dream he first got in contact with the psychological difficulty of moving from the conscious to the unconscious and hence the abnormal permeability of his contact barrier. When awake, this new first conquest finds a motor equivalent in the attempt to narrow the painful distance between himself and his mother. In deciding to maintain a perceptive register, I was also following the directives of the patient himself: I, too, must not become for him a suffocating presence but instead keep a certain distance and so await the onset of a more developed representative capacity for confronting the catastrophic separations which have marked his life.

A few sessions later, describing the process resulting from the dream, Mr F himself depicts his new ability to contact unthinkable emotions in a poetic way. 'You know', he says, 'it's as if a swarm of memories which I had forgotten had flown from my heart to my mind'.[20]

The expression of emotions implicit in the form

It was the experience of drawing with children that taught me to observe how form is created and to distinguish the emotions that inhabit it. As Tisseron[21] has suggested, the representation of the phantasy of a shared skin is precociously expressed in children through traces which establish contact, for instance, the traces they mark with their fingers in food spilled on the table. When the child begins to draw on the page, these primitive representations evolve into more symbolic elements, finite forms such as circles or spirals. In adults, traces of these old experiences remain in images or representations which privilege imprints over lines, or else in the imagination, through a way of thinking which makes use of the search for resemblances. Conversely, the fantasy of active control over separation produces traces of movement, such as dotted shapes and wavy or jagged lines. In adults, their evolution would correspond to drawings or paintings that privilege lines and, in imaginative terms, to evocative shapes.

An example taken from Western art history aptly illustrates what can also take place in the consulting room. In 1926, a Brâncuși bronze, *Bird in the Sky*, was seized by US customs officials and taxed as a manufactured good, with the justification that "*this stuff is not art*".[22] The officials' view that the bird was too abstract was echoed by New World art critics who regarded that sculpture as a jinx which announced a break with the old aesthetic canon. The evocative form produced a defensive reaction, first aesthetic and then juridical, which ended up generating a cultural debate that went beyond the case itself.

I find this example revealing of what can take place in the consulting room when we are not able to figure out whether the emotion beneath the form requires a strengthening of containment on the part of the analyst or, on the contrary, support in an evocative and hence transformative movement. This type of transducer of emotions and images, acquired through my work with children, has been a very useful instrument for understanding images produced by adults. It has enabled me to perceive the form of the different psychic movements beneath representations, both those produced in dreams and those produced in daydreams during a session, and to provide better responses.

Symptoms or regressions can also be seen as forms of development

Regressive phenomena are very frequent and do not in themselves amount to a phenomenon which coincides with the involution of the capacity for psychological work. Like many psychoanalysts, I have become used to thinking about them as coinciding with a greater oscillation characteristic of living beings, but it had never occurred to me that they could constitute a formal aspect of a kind of psychological 'concentration', capable of making the process develop.

Stefano is a five-year-old boy who draws very well for his age. At a certain point in his twice-weekly analysis, he starts to produce 'highly regressive' drawings, sketches filled with fragmentary lines, which leave me feeling very uneasy. I formulate many hypotheses in an attempt to understand what I could have introduced into the relationship to induce him to act younger than his age. My alarm is placated when he himself reveals the meaning of what is happening between us.

While drawing, Stefano says, 'I can't see. I can't see very well', or 'It's impossible to see this'.

It occurs to me that, through this sign, he might in part be seeking to focus on an event that was not so much traumatic as new, and this enables me to view what is happening as a progression.

Just as before the birth of a performative or psychological capacity, children are compelled laboriously to imagine what they do not know, and this concentration in focusing produces a macro photograph which blurs everything else, including already acquired capacities. Slightly unwittingly, I use what I had learnt from Stefano, the child discussed in the previous example, with the patient Mrs M.

After a period of well-being, Mrs M – in analysis three times a week for three years – once again suffers the paralyzing effect of panic attacks. Following several attempts to share with her a set of β elements, which I assume increase with her fear of going outdoors, I speak to her about her ability to be focused while working as an editor, correcting drafts and looking for syntactical errors or typos. I suggest that the type of concentration she uses at work and which little by little allows her to feel at one with what she sees, as she had previously told me, has something in common with her agoraphobia.

In this way, the things she would like to abolish end up being at one with certain external places. This new perspective, more focused on her ability to concentrate than on her pathology, enables her to focus on the numerous micro situations that give birth to hatred, a feeling which is unacceptable to her and often out of place.

Composition within relational space: a plastic way of expressing emotions tied to distance and nearness

When I listen to stories where there are signs of a spatial relationship, I inevitably think about how space is a primary reality, beginning from when the child deals with his going away from and coming back to his mother and then all the circumstances that could keep him away from her. Slightly unwittingly, I end up looking at the images that are formed in my mind in response to these stories in the same way as I would look at a drawing of a child – that is, considering the emotive meaning of the distance and nearness which determine the composition and the perspective.

Giuseppe has a twin sister, whom his parents consider much better than him at school and in life in general. At his first consultation, Giuseppe makes a drawing of his own family (see Figure 1.2).

Unable to make him out in the drawing, I ask if he is hidden. Giuseppe then makes a second drawing in which he is on the floor, in hibernation like an insect, but ready to climb up the ladder as soon as there is a mind out there capable of dreaming with him the feelings of exclusion and worthlessness which inhabit him (see Figure 1.3).

In his drawing, the desire to remain passive, to put intolerably painful emotions to rest – in short, to remain little – is mixed together with the desire to develop his ability to elaborate his emotions, a desire currently located outside himself, in the ladder.

Figure 1.2 The family of Giuseppe

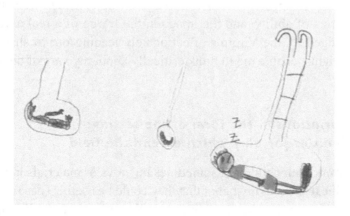

Figure 1.3 Giuseppe in hibernation like an insect

With adult patients, too, I have experienced on several occasions how, when dreaming or narrating a scene, the composition is not random but rather directly linked to the psychological distance in the relationship with their own internal objects and with me. In fact, this way of considering images from an aesthetic and emotional perspective has at times enabled me to encounter unconscious aspects of the field, aspects that therefore concern the patient and me while we seek to think about emotions together.

Mr P is an adult patient in analysis three times a week for a serious form of insomnia and vertigo. One day, he describes an episode in which he finds himself on a balcony on the fourth floor, terrified by the idea of taking a single step. A friend tries to help him but, by touching him, makes him even more agitated.

I am reminded of an image of a fresco by Lorenzo di Pietro in Siena in which the Virgin is depicted leaning out of a gap in the clouds. Her arms are holding a ladder which a few angels (children who have died young) are laboriously climbing. I describe the image to my patient and I tell him that, in order not to be frightened by heights, the following two ingredients are necessary: not a friend who touches but a mother who leans out lovingly and a ladder which bridges the gap between the ground and the sky.

Mr P is a very intelligent and sensitive man, and his mind intuitively grasps my allusion to how heights can describe the psychological distance from an object when this is simultaneously loved and hated and how they can take away the hope of reaching it and the capacity to work through one's emotions. Moreover, his description of the friend who in his daydream is apparently close to him but who considers herself above him in terms of ability, and the image in the fresco of a real asymmetry being bridged by the Virgin's affectionately leaning out to share in the fear of heights, enable me to think critically about my way of being close to him.

Small variations in the form of the setting: opportunities for play which extend the field

For my work with children, I sometimes buy toys or materials in response to a specific need or to my belief that they could be useful. These purchases once seemed to me to be an environmental response, in the Winnicottian sense, to psychological needs. In adult analysis, too, I have encountered, in the work of my colleagues, descriptions of concrete gestures carried out in the setting and considered in a similar way. For instance, while understanding as a psychological communication a patient's claim that he feels cold, the analyst can warm up the environment by raising the temperature a little before confronting with the patient his sense of his relational coldness. This kind of concrete gesture is a maternal, bodily response, useful and at times necessary for accessing the verbal sharing of the psychological coldness.

What has become clear to me through child analysis is that these gestures are carried out not just in response to the patient's needs. Ogden[23] has demonstrated that the analyst's associations or thoughts, supposedly external to the communication taking place, can also be daydreams capable of picking up on aspects as yet unthinkable in the analytic third and therefore in the analyst's and patient's joint unconscious. When I began imagining that these achievements could be a kind of dream of psychological aspects, present in the field and attached to the setting, they took on a different meaning in my work with both adults and children. Some gestures thus became not a variation of the setting but a narrative addition to it. It was the following episode that led me to this conclusion.

Tommaso is a four-year-old boy in analysis four times a week who is affected by a sort of evolutionary disharmony. About a month after the start of his therapy, I bought a fire engine for him. When in the play, he engages obsessively in the act of extinguishing me by drowning me in water. I manage to come into contact with my burning and pressing desire to extinguish his uncontainable movements around the room, produced by serious psychological burns. I accept the drowning of this desire, and the field is transformed.

Isomorphic or different mental operations?

I return now to the dialogue between the two sisters, which inspired the comparison between child and adult analysis. In response to an interlocutor who maintained that it was impossible for writers to render through writing the complexity of reality, including that of an emotional kind, Virginia Woolf replied that a modern writer can no longer be satisfied with the formal linearity of a sentence and that, at heart, painters and writers have to face common problems.

In the same way, psychoanalysts are primarily interested in tracing, through patients' stories or children's play, the expression of emotions and the complex way in which these are represented, whether they work with children or with adults.

Nevertheless, Virginia Woolf herself, in her essay 'Three Pictures', returns to reflecting on the relationship between painting and writing by warning against writers who paint reality like a painting and painters who attempt to tell stories. She thus advances the hypothesis that, while artists have common problems, their works should take on specific features in accordance with the materials of their trade. While for a writer the story is a central element of her art, a painter must paint objects through the emotions which these arouse, and the stories must be hidden in the paintings like *"mackerel behind the glass at the aquarium"*.[24]

I find this image very effective in showing how, in child analysis – in my opinion, closer to painting – the verbal decoding must be as far as possible hidden, and it is the vitality of play and its concrete taking shape through moving bodies that are the means of communication.

While in the adults' consulting room it is immobility which promotes a state of reverie, in that of children it is the body which constructs the dream, and this fact alters the kind of control which the analyst can maintain as the session unfolds. When I am with an adult, just as when writing, I know that every so often I can make use of moments of silence and reread with the patient – that is, go over the analytic dialogue through which we had attempted to work through unconscious emotions. The rhythm of the interaction allows my mind to immerse itself and re-emerge fairly rhythmically from the profound emotional sharing. As I have sought to describe, the interaction flows differently with a child; the immersion which takes place through doing things together lasts longer, and reflection is often possible only in après-coup. Play, more than language, contains what cannot be formalized and achieves, through a process of rapid transformations, the category of potentiality and the acquisition of a sensitivity which allows the child to create new parts of himself.

The practice of child analysis induces in the therapist a more intense sensitivity towards rhythmic and formal features, which can yield new perspectives on adult analysis. From the complex processes described here, I have extracted a few features which have influenced and altered my analytic work with adults. Such examples revolve around a different, more mature sensitivity towards the sensorial features which sketch the form of the representation before it becomes properly such; I have learnt better to identify emotions which imply forms, distinguishing those which privilege print and which refer to evocative forms from those which instead privilege closed forms, which refer to resemblances. In other examples, I have sought to demonstrate how aspects of relationships such as distance and closeness, when observed from a formal perspective, can enable a restitution to the patient of underlying emotions, differing from what I am able to do when I use reflective thought tied to language.

In conclusion, I highlighted how small, concrete acts within the setting could be understood by acquiring a particular perspective through one's work with children. The difference in the kind of interactions that take place in the two consulting rooms seems to me therefore not only to involve a difference in technique but also to end up influencing the way in which thoughts are formed: through reverie, associations, memories, figurative or literary allusions in the adults' consulting room; through actions, attention to form and spatial relationships, the imaginative use of objects, the use of the body in the children's consulting room and thus through forms close to a *logos* in the making, a *logos* generated by the living body.

In a short story by Ian McEwan, there is a particularly effective synthesis of the conflict which has animated the comparison between child and adult psychoanalysis and a synthesis of my thoughts regarding their possible relationship: "*Often they [Kate and Peter] kept the peace by drawing an imaginary line from the door right across their bedroom. Kate's side there, Peter's side here. . . . The invisible line worked well when they remembered about it. . . . It worked well enough until one wet Sunday afternoon they had a row, one of their worst, about where exactly this line was*".[25]

Child and adult analysis are not divided by a genuine boundary. As with Kate and Peter's room, there exists an imaginary line that divides them, not an impenetrable line but a fluid boundary that may be penetrated with the other's permission. However, the temptation to do away with the boundary, as history demonstrates, brings with it certain dangers. Indeed, recognizing their diversity helps define their uniqueness, and articulating this difference gives life to a creative dialogue and a genuine reciprocity. In this sense, the small waiting room which unites and divides the two consulting rooms in my office has taken on a metaphorical significance for me and thus fills me with curiosity and fascination: it is the place where, in a kind of crossing over, there is a meeting and exchange of fragments of my approach to adult and child analysis.

Notes

1 Woolf 1944, p. 77. Excerpt from 'Lappin and Lappinova' from A HAUNTED HOUSE AND OTHER SHORT STORIES by Virginia Woolf. Copyright 1944 by Houghton Mifflin Harcourt Publishing Company. Copyright © renewed 1972 by Houghton Mifflin Harcourt Publishing Company. Reprinted with permission of Houghton Mifflin Harcourt Publishing Company. All rights reserved.

2 Mahon 2000, p. 136. For the inner relationship between art and the psychoanalytic process, see also Civitarese 2014, Nicholsen 2015.
3 Woolf 1994, p. 493.
4 Freud 1914. See also Harold Blum's article reviewing the literature about the only case around a child by Freud (Blum 2007).
5 Klein 1932.
6 Wangh 1950.
7 The question of the relationship between the arts was taken up by the philosopher Jacques Derrida. Rejecting the dominant cultural position, Derrida maintained that painting was the highest art form (a simulacrum, the very location of a truth still unknown to the deceptive order of discourse), then writing, which derives value not from its affiliation with *logos* but with image, and finally the word, a castaway in a sea of polysemy. See Baraldi et al. 1996, p. 9.
8 See Bion's works: 1962a, 1965, 1970.
9 Bion 1967, p. 143.
10 Joseph 1998. For a larger view on Kleinian technique, see also Joseph 1989.
11 Winnicott 1971, p. 41.
12 Winnicott 1971.
13 Frankel 1998, Gaines 1995, Krimendahl 1998, Slade 1994.
14 Beebe and Lachmann 2003, Knight 2003, Stern 1977, Stern et al. 1998.
15 Ferro 2004, Ogden 1985, 2001.
16 Bonoviz 2004.
17 Milner 1950.
18 Ferro and Basile 2006, p. 489.
19 Di Renzo and Nastasi 1989. Di Renzo and Nastasi observed that the children could shift from their bodies to something more abstract. They almost could understand from a falling ball the physics laws of dynamic equations, like speed and sequence of time.
20 Anzieu-Premmereur 2016. Christine Anzieu in a therapy with a young boy uses the Federn's discovery to support her hypothesis that the dreamer remains in unified contact with the breast and that this determines constant characteristics of the dream, such as the dream screen. In her as in my patient, the nightmare that broke up sleeping can be seen as a first attempt to dream the primitive agonies that Winnicott described as a way to deal with dissociation.
21 Tisseron 1993, 1994, p. 40.
22 See Edelman 2001.
23 Ogden 2007.
24 Woolf 1964, p. 142. In 1923, Vanessa Bell illustrated her sister's novel "Kew Gardens". The sketches became part of the pages, starting from the first letter and ending as a puzzle with all the words. This is almost like a model of the child and adult relationship in psychoanalysis. Woolf 1921, p. 9 and p. 13.
25 McEwan 1994, pp. 24–26. Excerpted from *The Daydreamer* by Ian McEwan. Copyright © 1995 Ian McEwan. Published by Jonathan Cape. Reprinted with permission of The Random House Group Limited and Doubleday Canada, a division of Penguin Random House Canada Limited.

Chapter 2

Luigi and the cinématographe, the first motion-picture camera

> Everyone's childhood memories consist, I think, of a number of visual impressions, of which many are very clear but don't have any chronological sense.
>
> Giuseppe Tomasi di Lampedusa[1]

On 22 March 1895, Luis Lumière presented the results of his invention to the audience: the cinématographe. Legend has it that Lumière discovered the principle of motion pictures by watching his mother sewing on a machine. By adapting the sewing machine mechanism called presser-foot to his device, he solved the tricky problem of dragging fixed images on a tape, recreating a story by images and solving the problem of putting together continuous and discontinuous movement and immobility.

I will borrow the ingredients of this story to talk about some aspects of an analytic treatment with a child I will call Luigi.

In the interview with his parents, his mother told me that since his infancy Luigi had been a 'fearful boy'. He was cautious in his movements and in exploring the environment because he was always afraid of hurting himself. Sleeping by himself was a step he had hardly achieved at home. Paradoxically, Luigi didn't have any problem when he went on holiday by himself. At the time of the interview, Luigi was eleven years old, and for about three years, he had been performing small rituals to fall asleep, but now they had become 'too many'. He was terrified that some thieves would break into the house and kill him, that the electricity, running the household appliances, could start a fire. So, at night, he had to get up countless times to check that the TV set or the computer were unplugged, that the windows were locked and that the alarm was on. During the day, he was exhausted and had a headache all the time. As he attempted to meet his parents' expectations, Luigi asked them to make a lot of changes in his bedroom. His parents tried to meet his requests, as if they wanted to compensate, by this actual mobility, Luigi's tendency to immobility. His parents were also able to intuitively understand a link between their child's current bizarre behaviour and the difficulty characterizing his infancy. In particular, his mother told me that she felt as if 'the thread of their relationship had become entangled', and she understood the need for some help so that Luigi could again invest energy in the direction of his development and creativity.

The background of a meeting

Anzieu[2] describes how, at the beginning of the psychic life, the child has to create representations of the configuration of the body and the objects in space as well as their movements. These representations stem from the crossroads of very primitive bodily and relational sensations that precede actual representations and can therefore be more appropriately called formal signifiers.

Starting from Tisseron's intuition,[3] he develops it by defining these proto-representations as patterns and identifying two types: containment and transformation patterns.

Containment patterns arise from the introjection of pleasant experiences of care, such as looking into the eyes of the other person, being held or being cradled; transformation patterns rely on the experience of the exchanges with the mother or the maternal environment and can be skin-to-skin experiences or experiences that involve striated muscles or articular or breathing movements. As the rudimentary ego owns these patterns, they become the underpinning for more complex fantasy representations. Tisseron says that an overinvestment of the enveloping (containment) patterns lays the foundation for obsessive neurotic manifestations, such as the ones from which Luigi suffered.

The patterns that each person prefers become more visible every time a psychic danger is involved, and they manifest themselves actively in the transference. Their emergence is also a sign of the first step towards their potential transformation, if we are able to take the opportunity to describe this form before its content.

I want to focus on the very form of the patterns and their vicissitudes in the analytic field. As they cannot rely on a real mental functioning, which is the result of an internalization process, the containment patterns appear particularly clear in terms of relationship or some features of the figurative representation that seems to be at a much more primitive level than the verbal one.

What I am interested in trying to describe is the form of the containment pattern enacted in the relationship at the beginning of analysis and its transformations until the birth and development of Luigi's passion for the cinema, which actually occurred as an effect of his three-year analytic treatment and as concrete evidence of the appearance of new transformation patterns.

I will try to highlight this creative transformation through his drawings and the progressive emergence inside me of interpretative interventions that were qualitatively different over time.

Here I use the word *birth*, as I want to underline that it was not only the appearance of new facts but also a physical and psychic co-experience of transformation which had its core in a body experience, as in the biological realm. It seemed to me that the possibility of first grasping the shape in the relationship and then in the representations stood both for Luigi and for myself at the crossroads of a movement of identification with the shape of the primal relationship in its bodily specificity and as projective movements with overt bodily implications similar to those of artistic representation.

The sound of the sewing machine

Relying on the relational premise that seems to have been at the basis of the invention of the cinema, we can imagine that the first ingredient of this creative synthesis might have been the internalization of the rhythmical sound envelope created by the repetitive gesture of the mother. I think that the reconstruction of the sound rhythm also represented the first step for Luigi and myself.

The lack of rhythm was one of the first sensations I was able to identify. At first, Luigi did not agree to play or draw; he did not resort to any motor activity to explore the environment and always sat up properly in the chair where he had sat the first time we met. For some months, he talked about himself continuously during the entire time available to him. Luigi was setting up a highly evolved symbolic representation where his words seemed to keep a potentially life-threatening void away. This was something very similar to Scheherazade's stories, where the end of the stories meant the death of the storyteller. What became progressively clear to me was that words could not be an appropriate means to come into touch with this fear. Those rare times when I somewhat forcefully entered his stories, Luigi smiled and did not respond to my intervention.

In hindsight, I think that my interpretations tried somehow to push, with a machine of theories, the relational fabric before the fabric literally took shape between the two of us. Like Lumière's mother, I had to accept sewing by myself without feeling anxious because I was being observed.

Only in hindsight was I able to think about the special quality of the role Luigi gave me as a substitute of the primary object. His storytelling without any pauses and without a rhythm created a sound envelope around him that ritualized a very primitive situation in the transference and also put me in a territory where it was not easy to recover word presentations.[4]

At the beginning of his life, Luigi had experienced an excessive presence, as his mother had probably been too anxious – because of the physical experience of a depleted body and the ensuing depression that its mentalization implies – and had organized her own healing by being helped by seven women who were supposed to ensure the non-void with care and attention.

For this child, the relationship could be established only by asking me to adhere to the form of his first transformational object.

If, as Bollas[5] says, the object becomes such not so much through desire but through perceptive identification with its function, in the transference, the delicate problem of finding some point of harmony stood between the two of us. This point of harmony should then allow for the structuring of a psychic container capable of resonating, recognizing the rhythm of presence and absence – which was probably missing at the beginning of the child's life.

The main problem of my relationship with Luigi was to perceive and then describe the shape of something too full – which happened through the void becoming present.

One day, lulled by the warm and continuous flow of his words, I realized that I was falling asleep, and with a startle, a memory came to mind because of a similar feeling. One night, a light weight on my knees made me aware that, in falling asleep, my daughter had slid out of my arms.

An early awareness of some painful void appeared in me. That void involved both my identification with an infant and my countertransference imbued with narcissistic and aggressive feelings that somehow brought me close to the maternal experience.

I think that this sequence actualized, in my relationship with Luigi, the form of his early relationship with his mother that tended to deny his experience of discontinuity and void.

The sensation of falling met the feeling of void through the memory of my body experience. I think that my interpretation stemmed from this specific feeling. I said to him that, as I was about to tell him something, I had the sensation that my words fell inside, just like when you are held in someone's arms and you are dropped. An unpleasant sensation.

After this event, a rhythm gradually and mysteriously developed between us. At some point, I realized that we had a good session, although I had hardly spoken a word. I realized that feeling observed had not annoyed me and that my listening was paced on his words. I think that this first structuring had to do with the psychic capacity to match with the pulsating rhythm of biological paces and with an early arrangement of coordination and synchronization of the different elements of the psychic apparatus, some sort of internal organization that makes them compatible with the rhythm and, ultimately, with the representation of time.[6]

The fabric as a prototype of the screen

Many times, Luigi, when he saw the pieces of paper and the markers on the table, had explained that he did not know how to draw and did not want to. Two months after these statements, he told me that, if I gave him a piece of squared paper, he would show me what he had learned to do in technical studies classes with set squares. This is why he absolutely had to have a piece of squared paper.

The first prototype of a blank screen appeared. He could project his first representations on it. The small squares made the image of containment come alive – a containment that had developed by layers, session after session and through our unconscious thoughts crossing one another. By accurately following the lines, Luigi made his first drawing (see Figure 2.1).

The drawing itself depicted the same representation of a space made up of many small spaces – perhaps a representation of his own specific containment pattern. Its shape had become more concrete in the transference relationship. Now the rhythmical sound of the sewing machine had its visual equivalent in many compressed small frames – still depleted

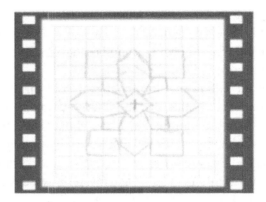

Figure 2.1 First drawing on a squared paper

of representation. However, his ability to trace a shape by leaning carefully on the edges of the small squares showed, as I saw it, the first seeds of transformation and of his creativity, based on a specific sensitivity for pictures. Lumière watched his mother sewing and internalized a specific skill through her gestures. He observed his mother's body, which moved rhythmically. This probably re-actualized for him some comforting experiences, such as being cradled, and re-established the affective bridge that enables the artist to overcome the distress implied in the first mark left on a blank screen. He observed the up-and-down motion of the needle, some sort of fort-da game. He watched how a line on the fabric created a shape.

The shape of the seam and the first images

Within a one-year time frame, the relational fabric between us seemed to have a sufficient extension to start sewing. What I call the relational fabric can also be understood as the shape of an internalized container. The initial density of the words, as an enactment of a continual self-induced stimulation in order to shun the anxiety of the void, had diluted. His first drawing testified to a more symbolic sketched transcription of body fantasies and unconscious ghosts.

Sometimes Luigi drew silently for himself to design defensive systems for his room. I observed him and imagined that the little characters appearing here and there expressed small representational clusters, but I still could not give a name to it all.

At one point, I found myself observing them in a special way. I was in a state of mind similar to when one is drawing. It is almost impossible to draw by focusing on the object one wants to represent. It is much better to focus on the outside shape of the object and the empty spaces surrounding it. To do so, one needs to shift to a different kind of concentration and activate a different attention from the one we use to perceive the spatial arrangement of the objects. We are engrossed in our activity, and that dislocated attention triggers some sort of perception free from the use and the function of the objects. Marion Milner describes a similar focus which she calls *"concentration of the body"*.[7] As I focused on the void, I was challenged by my fighting against oversaturated interpretations in order to be able to stay on the boundary of the potential birth of new meaning. At other times, as I was trying to visualize the shape traced by the line, and I was observing it along its external contour, I felt I was filled with the intimate pleasure of a game I used to play countless times during my childhood – that is, giving clouds a symbolic shape.

So, I tried to focus on my feeling as I was observing the small and somewhat obsessive drawings that Luigi kept on producing (see Figure 2.2).

I thought back to the game of the clouds and the pleasure it also gave me by virtue of an underlying omnipotent fantasy. After all, I experienced that I was 'creating' anything that came to mind as long as it was emotionally invested enough that it could be projected onto the backdrop of the sky. I also felt puzzled because that game, which had been so easy when I was

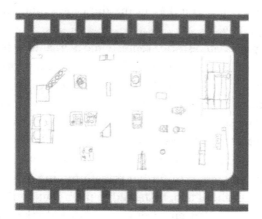

Figure 2.2 Furniture and alarm systems in Luigi's room

a child, was now screened by a more critical consciousness that seized differences and incongruous details between what I saw and the representation of the object as it was symbolically stored in my memory.

This was the feeling, strongly mediated by visual impressions, that brought me into contact with a thought. Luigi also had to use his omnipotent fantasy to create the mother and found her again as an object inside and outside himself.[8] But the continual turnover of 'mothers', the succession of smiles, different somatic traits and many different ways of taking care might have generated in him at first confusion and later an intimate fear to explore outside reality through his eyes. Consequently, the feeling that moving was something dangerous had developed inside him.

I said, 'You know, while you are drawing I see many small objects, maybe traps, but I don't see the enemy. I think that the enemy is hiding, maybe it takes on many different faces and that is why he confuses us. You are scared he might hit us. At times, you would really like to kill him, but actually we don't know what he looks like, and we need to build many things to protect us without ever being sure that they are effective defences'.

Some experiments of short sequences

Following this episode, Luigi started to talk about a new video game he loved. It was about exploring and colonizing a territory bristling with dangers. In this way, the enemies popped up, took shape and could be fought with the 'Big Daddy' catapult. There were also scenes that overtly concerned the bodies. Like in a dream, the thing-presentation appeared, and the ghosts took shape.

The computer-animated stories represented a great leap forward towards the conquest and the endogenous formation of a transformation pattern. Luigi could keep control over the pattern of images of the video game through strategies of defence and fleeing that allowed him to explore new and dangerous landscapes where he was willing to venture.

An explicit reference to the body – feeling empty and full through nourishment – was condensed in an anomalous drawing for that time and that looked like a precursor of further transformation.

One day, after a school trip, he talked to me about a gift he had bought for his parents: a wooden cup from which one drinks directly through some small slots (see Figure 2.3).

Figure 2.3 'Grolla' or crafted cup

The drawing was anomalous in its round shape and because of the dawning idea of a couple (parents, he and I) that could drink together. That drinking together seemed very meaningful, in light of his history.

After the wooden cup, the video-game stories continued and allowed further meanings to develop. The full and empty spaces were no longer only associated with the digestive function.

The elements of an incipient genital sexuality that appeared in his drawings became clearer, and his first representations became richer in emotions linked to his fantasizing about promontories and narrow gorges of more human landscapes.

The dread of a destructive phallus from the ancient symbiosis persisted, but at the same time, elements of identification with the father and his function started to be established.

Then, at some point, a new formal element appeared: the frame.

From the external screen to the internal one

In art, the presence of a frame, that can sometimes be a limit of the piece of paper itself, marks the boundary between what needs to be interpreted realistically and what belongs to the symbolic game. For Luigi, it marked the accomplishment of a restructuring of his psychic container. Once he had repaired the largest leaks, he could now let go of the desire for a fusion without signs and the dread of exploring the symbolic area which was too uncertain. I was reminded of Ella Sharpe's teaching,[9] as she writes about a strongly inhibited patient who was able to decrease his aggressive desires and the linked sense of death. She wrote that his body ego needed to be preserved and helped to develop, and its function emerged only by letting fantasies about the body.

Until then, Luigi's drawings looked flat and lacked all reference to different planes.

I was amazed and deeply moved when one evening he told me that at school they had had to draw a castle. Whereas his schoolmates drew it in a conventional manner, from the front, he had the idea of drawing a castle with a house inside it. In front of me, my astonished eyes saw an aesthetically very beautiful and complex representation taking shape (see Figure 2.4).

A house inside a castle, a defensive frame protecting an intimate place and intimate affections. That evening, Luigi again found, in his unconscious, his connections between the frame and the feeling of being held and contained in his mother's arms as well as feeling the intimate enjoyment of such an experience.

I think that this surprisingly beautiful shape has the value of a real creation of art in Luigi's history, where there is an aesthetic merging in the symbolic shape of the loved (form) and feared (content) object.[10]

Figure 2.4 House inside a castle

Twenty-four frames per second

In the last year we spent together, Luigi drew a lot. He illustrated stories and comics but mostly movies and gradually developed a passion for motion pictures. His fear of moving dissipated, and the pleasure associated with this event was condensed in a drawing of a machine to learn how to dance. He had seen it during a trip with his grandparents, and he had observed its functioning carefully because he had found it was an extraordinary invention. On a sort of large screen on the floor, a numerical sequence appeared, and one was supposed to step on it. Keeping the rhythm, this exercise turned into a dance.

He drew the machine. The first thing that occurred to me was the pedal of my grandmother's sewing machine and the rhythm it produced, a very similar rhythm to the one of dancing.

It became clear to me that the entire analytic process had been supported by an affective investment that had been played out particularly in body sensations and the pleasure of rediscovering playing and drawing, as another form of playing.

The machine to learn how to dance, with its rhythmic background, brings me back to the initial story that helped me think about this child analysis. I will use it again to try to clarify some of its salient aspects.

The analytic relationship wove a set of shared meanings between Luigi and myself. These meanings developed from intense moments, mostly made up of images and body sensations. I like to think of this sequence of such moments as some sort of seam.

A seam is made of stitches, visible units and empty spaces. The empty spaces are produced by the needle that goes through the fabric itself, fixes the stitches to a thread placed on the side underneath, the underground side. This thread does not appear except in its function of creating discontinuity. Now, I think that the unconscious elements of the two of us produced these 'creative' discontinuities. Like a seam, this child analysis was built upon more visible elements, such as his drawings, his daily stories and in the transference, but also along a sequence of sensations associated with being-not being, full-empty, visible-invisible.

At first, the countertransference sensation of the possibility of being dropped or of not being firmly held allowed the lack, which Luigi had experienced at his birth and had probably contributed to the formation of his defective containment pattern, to come into play.

Later, a kind of common skin developed between us and enabled us to focus on a similar sensation but more connected with the body parts and their functions. The sensation of full and empty went through the digestive, visual and finally sexual functions. The containment patterns settled gradually, and the transformation patterns could develop until they were manifested in the body, in the pleasure of moving and dancing.

It seems to me that even though the whole body, with its sensations associated with its various functions, was involved, a key part was played by looking, both in this analysis and in Mr Lumière's story. For a child, looking up at the mother's face and breast is such a fundamental sensory affective experience that it is assimilated with the self, as Anzieu[11] put it.

Particularly for Luigi, to re-establish a fixed place to stare at, as a counterbalance to the turnover of his many mothers, was a necessity to be able to recover his psychic development.

Once he found the object visually, Luigi could explore it and this event became clear, as the aesthetic object organized the emergence of the first transformational pattern in the transference.

Later, his being able to stare at and feel the void enabled Luigi to draw a line that, in a perspective view, progressively defined the contours of an aesthetically beautiful symbolic drawing and enabled him to access his creative capacity.

Thinking back to Lumière, I thought that in the sequence of images it is the very short interval of empty spaces, of lack of vision, that produces the sensation of pictures in motion.

So, his analysis, like the presser-foot, produced some seams and allowed Luigi to bring together continuity and discontinuity, movement and immobility in himself.

Notes

1 Tomasi di Lampedusa 1961, p. 26. Reprinted with permission of Giangiacomo Feltrinelli Editore.
2 Anzieu 1985.
3 Decobert and Sacco 1995, pp. 121–137.
4 Racalbuto 1994, p. 66.
5 Bollas 1987, pp. 13–29.
6 Sugarman 2003.

7 Milner 1950, p. 127. See also Stern 1974.
8 Winnicott 1986.
9 Sharpe Freeman 1978. From a different theoretical prospective, Hobson highlights how emotionally grounded sharing of experiences, not merely or predominantly intentions, is critical for the development of interpersonal understanding. Such sharing entails forms of self-other connectedness and differentiation that are essential to communication and symbolic functioning and reorient a subjective attitude (Hobson and Meyer 2005).
10 Stokes 1955. See also the interesting thought around the relationship between sensation and creative forms in Charles 2001.
11 Anzieu 1985.

Chapter 3

An analyst learns to play
From crumpled-up paper to origami

> The playing field can be made up of any material and foundation apart from soft grass. It should have at least one part on gravel, at least one obstacle such as a tree or a boulder, a slope with a gradation as steep as twenty per-cent, at least one muddy puddle and it should not be fenced off, but should possibly be situated somewhere where the ball could roll away for a few miles if it were kicked out of the field.
>
> Stefano Benni[1]

In my mind, the idea of the bi-personal field[2] is always associated, more or less consciously, with the image of the lines of force between the positive and negative poles of an electromagnetic field, rendered visible by iron filings. This image is useful to visually represent the interaction that creates the psychoanalytic field, but at the same time, it does not do justice to the complex and unpredictable dynamic through which the interpersonal field is produced and developed in a fluctuating way over time. The imaginative form with which the idea of the analytic field was associated in my mind had a chance to grow when I learned of Dr Koryo Miura's story.[3]

Miura was an aerospace engineer who, while working on a NASA shuttle project in the 1980s, had studied the distortion of shuttles and the system of folding to the antennae of space probes; the perpendicular folding of these instruments caused a series of problems related to instability and excessive wear and tear along the lines of closure. Thus, the structural support often ended up compromising the use of the instrument itself. In studying this problem, he became interested in the phenomenon of crumpling (starting with the apparently simple act of crumpling paper) and asked himself what determined the irregularity of the folds, what the particular resistance of some of them was and what might be the dependent relationship between the extent of the surface and the previously mentioned folds. He found a brilliant solution to this type of structural problem by drawing inspiration from the ancient art of origami and realizing that, for the support of the antennae, a slanted fold was much less wearing than perpendicular ones. Seeking further information, I discovered that, despite his colleagues' perplexity about the utility of this research, Professor Miura initially succeeded in furthering his studies thanks to an Italian company that asked him to apply his preliminary observations to the improved folding of a topographical map, putting into effect a way of folding that was very similar to that of origami. A map made in this way was not only very easy to open and close but also the slant folds ended up much less worn than the perpendicular ones. This idea of a map, which in and of itself describes places and borders, and to which a further fold is applied that in turn traces and defines new borders, became a visual suggestion that helped me better imagine the analytic field.

I felt myself in the throes of a similar problem in the analysis of Giacomo, a child in treatment for psychological difficulties that arose following numerous operations he had undergone for a congenital rectal atresia. Considering Miura's proposal for the refolding of antennae in the light of feelings that I experienced in this child's analysis led me to an initial way of conceiving the nature of our difficulties, permitting me to identify a dangerous friction precisely at the point of contact between something of mine and something of his. This feeling of danger appeared to me in some moments of the analysis like a sudden crumpling up and at other times like an insidious deterioration. Following the creative idea of the origami with which Miura had resolved his problem, it seemed to me that what had been occurring less frequently was in fact the creative capacity to fold or bend ourselves to play. I asked myself whether, in reflecting on some situations that I had perceived as critical, I might better understand which elements generated our play and which could make me aware of its deterioration.

Hypotheses on analytic play

Ogden[4] demonstrated that Winnicott and Bion, though elaborating two very different theoretical perspectives, shared a particular interest in the way in which the mind develops from the body within the primary relationship. Winnicott described how the integrity of psychic development can be guaranteed by the maternal capacity to protect the child from a traumatic discontinuity, until the child can develop a sense of himself as separate and can creatively participate in the relationship. An early form of this creative participation was described by Winnicott as an index of the capacity to play and the space where this occurs as transitional space.[5] Bion saw the same phenomenon from the viewpoint of the working through of unconscious emotions, describing how the mother helps the child develop a container that can dream unconscious emotions. A contact barrier is constructed that can regulate the emotional, conscious-unconscious flow in an optimal way, both intrasubjectively and in the intersubjective field.[6] Ogden,[7] uniting Winnicott's concept of transitional space and the subjective use of the object with that of Bion's container-contained, hypothesized that in the analytic relationship, a third space can be constructed: the intersubjective third of analysis, co-constructed by both subjects of the analysis, in which analyst and analysand project their own subjective, unconscious vision of self and other. The two subjectivities relate to each other in this area within a dynamic tension. Elaborating on Ogden's idea that play can be considered a conscious-unconscious *"joint construction"*[8] of the analytic couple, I hypothesize that some of its characteristics can be seen as a sort of conscious emotional derivative of the intersubjective contact barrier's functioning inside the area of the analytic third. Although I am borrowing the term *"narrative derivatives"* from Ferro, I am using it here with a slightly different meaning. Ferro[9] hypothesized that the narrations, the play, the auditory or visual sensations that the patient introduces into the analytic field may be a conscious manifestation of the unconscious work carried out by the couple to metabolize the emotions that are continually generated in the analytic interaction. I hypothesize that some of the conscious emotional feelings described by Winnicott as characteristic of play can be utilized as indicators of the good functioning of the analytic process and in particular of the good functioning of the intersubjective contact barrier in the space of the analytic third. Contrary to the appearance of a character, which can be considered a rather precise response to the dialogue between analyst and patient,[10] some of the feelings connected to play may reflect the functioning of the intersubjective contact barrier, a function that is structured and restructured in a variable climate, not as an exact or immediate reaction. In my first clinical synopsis, I intend to describe how the pleasure of playing together gradually disappeared from the analytic relationship due to the gathering of emotions that were difficult to work through. That difficulty culminated in my attribution of it to the patient through the mental formulation of a psychopathological hypothesis. The nosological framing of a psychic disturbance can be an element of knowledge for the analyst beyond the session. Within the session, in contrast, this type of thought almost always constitutes, in my opinion, the analyst's extreme defence against intolerable emotions.

A challenge in the field: the process of crumpling up

When Giacomo first came to me for an analytic treatment three times a week, he had just turned six. During his first three years of life, he had suffered through many surgical interventions due to the rectal agenesis with which he was born. From that time onward, his face had been deformed by a series of tics accompanied by the emission of guttural sounds that were signs of his difficulty in being able to express in words or other more symbolic forms the anxiety and rage produced by the surgical events. As soon as he entered the playroom, Giacomo took a piece of paper from the table, crumpled it up, and began to kick it from one foot to the other and then to make it fly up high and hit the wall, continually calling my attention to his prowess. I thought that it might be important for him to show me an extraordinary skill of his in order to deal with his humiliating sense of bodily impotence, since he was still unable to hold back his faeces. This situation exposed him to serious social humiliation made even more acute by the fact that, at his elementary school – in contrast to his preschool – none of the other children needed assistance in going to the bathroom. Once it seemed to me that an emotionally appropriate situation was being created, I tried to speak with him about the difficulty that we were experiencing: the feeling of being rejected and of having to make a great effort to be favourably regarded. I spoke to him of my favourite sports team, of the feelings I had when they lost and when a player got expelled from the field. I tried to speak with him in that way, remaining close to his way of playing, about the experience of being overwhelmed by the cause of his difficulties and the consequent loss of his feeling healthy and capable of relating. There was an acknowledgment in my words that to some extent this experience seemed to be reproduced in me.

At times, Giacomo stopped for a moment and seemed to listen, but then he started up again, saying only, 'Come on, let's play!' In this early period of the analysis, Giacomo's play was a kind of excited and compulsive game, a format that could signal his difficulties in entering into real play. Inside me, too, it happened that Giacomo's invitation to play obscured his ambiguity about a sincere invitation, and at the same time, it hid the difficulty in the relationship. Instead of 'Come on, let's play!' I ended up feeling I had heard something like 'Shut up!' This first bending or folding in the relationship, of which I was unaware, set things up such that, with increasing frequency, I attributed difficulties in listening and in using words only to the child. Giacomo played in silence and primarily engaged in a continuous contest with himself. His challenges were to keep the little ball level for a greater number of kicks, to kick it five times without moving and so on. When he grew tired of this game, he began to run – 'as part of my training', he told me. In reality, it seemed to me that he was losing himself in total isolation, and the situation appeared much more serious than I had at first hypothesized. In the session, I had thought that Giacomo could be expressing some autistic traits through these relational withdrawals.

After some months, during a session in which I had felt particularly exhausted, the idea came to me to run together with Giacomo, without saying anything, as though my capacity to establish proximity could not be expressed in words in that moment but only in an imitative way. After a fit of rushing around, I stopped myself suddenly and sat down on the floor, gripped by a feeling of malaise. Giacomo joined me, stepping over me. He did this several times. Looking up, I saw him pass in front of me, his face contorted by tics. It was a crumpled-up face – like the ball of paper that he had constructed by scrunching up a sheet of paper and then kicking it around, I thought. 'If you want to run away, then you'll need a horse', I told him after some minutes of intense malaise, and I got onto all fours, inviting him with this gesture to climb onto my back. He was a bit perplexed but then settled himself on my back. I got up and, keeping him against my back, I began to run around the table. Fortunately, Giacomo was a small and delicate child, so I could run for the remainder of the session, resting every now and then and letting him know in advance of the stops. In the next session, he asked me to again 'play horsey'. The only thing I succeeded in feeling in the session was that this game restored a sense of pleasurable psycho-bodily contact. Only after the session did

I succeed in tracing the personal, painful meaning that had probably accompanied the game's inception. In offering myself to Giacomo as a horse, I had arranged things so that my body assumed a subordinated position. At the same time, in the phrase 'if you want to run away' with which I had introduced the offer, I was aware of having also spoken of my wish to rid myself of the sense of impotence that Giacomo – and particularly the persistence of his facial contractions – caused me to experience. I remembered how my mother often used to express her dissent about some of my choices through similar expressions, while with words she asserted my freedom to choose according to my own judgment. This way of contradicting what was being declared in words with a nonverbal message engendered a sense of painful uncertainty in me, and it made me experience an anger that would have had greater legitimacy in the face of an open prohibition. My giving up what I had wanted often became an affective necessity, but it also cut off my capacity to express either my thoughts or my feelings.

I developed the theory that the overlapping of some unconscious aspects of our particular histories had produced a deterioration of our capacity to remain engaged in play.

An early folding towards play

Giacomo had tried to use me as a *"subjective object"*[11] – that is, as an object subjectively invested with his emotions and thus as one not completely separate. However, having failed to find in me an environment that could respond adequately to his requests, due to my unconscious difficulties, he had mobilized a reaction that had also blocked a portion of his creative potential. The living image of the horse that suddenly arose in the field was what immediately appeared to me as the invention that seemed to have launched a transformation. This image had been given substance in my mind, utilizing a feeling belonging to my personal history; it had the characteristic of having arisen from the body and of having achieved a place of bodily and psychic encounter between analyst and patient, as happens between mother and child at the beginning of emotional development. It could emerge only when my childishness had succeeded in locating an initially imitative form (our running together) and then a form of working through the unconscious pain that Giacomo's face aroused in me.

Giacomo had contributed to this transformation because, with his body, he had provided me with an early pre-representation of how it was possible to run away from an aggressive doctor and from a mother who wasn't protective, which I represented for him in that moment. His running away had unconsciously introduced into the field the possibility of a very early transformation of the sense of paralysis in which we had been immersed.

Through imitating his gesture, I had authorized and listened to my own desire to run away as well, leaving space for an early iconic form of unconscious working through that made its entrance into the field as the image of a horse. This was revealed not only as an early transformation of my pain but also as a fantasy that correlated with a bodily sensation that could be used to explore the analytic third.[12] Indeed, sensations and body-related fantasies are the principal medium through which the analytic third is plumbed.

Subsequent to that day, Giacomo continued to suggest the 'horsey game' for some weeks, but after having become more aware of some of my emotions, I found myself experiencing a different feeling with respect to this repetition. While at first when Giacomo played ball in a repetitive way, I had seen this as a relational withdrawal, repeating the horsey game now seemed to me to be a necessary form of taking in and processing the traumatic unpredictability that Giacomo had experienced in relation to his body. Being able to predict my response allowed him, as it would the very young child, to build a form of security and trust in his own capacities to remain connected, a pre-reflective way of resonating with what cannot yet be known and therefore of containing it.[13]

From my point of view, the horsey game was also an expression of a creative capacity of mine, and Giacomo's request to continue playing it was a confirmation of our having met up with each other in the space of the analytic third. Thinking of the spatial probe as a metaphor for the analytic probe, I focused on the fact that both Miura and I had had to come to grips with an analogous problem: how to avoid repetitive actions wearing out the setting precisely at the point of articulation. After an actual crumpling up in the analytic field, the solution of perpendicular folding made it visually apparent that functioning became easier when the surfaces did not perfectly overlap – or rather, that after being overlapped, they could optimally interact in a slanted spatial or analytically transitional configuration. This latter possibility was actualized when Giacomo and I succeeded in experiencing through the body an initial sense of being in step together, and this had been evident through the restoration in play of a feeling of nourishment and mutual pleasure. Furthermore, an early hint of trust was born in me that Giacomo was capable of creatively using repetition.

The mail game and the expansion of the field

About two years later, Giacomo had become more capable of doing things in the relationship with me and I with him; the tics and the guttural sounds that distorted his communications were nearly gone.

Going back to playing with a ball, he had assigned me the role of goalkeeper, such that I alone had the experience of suffering the consequences of a goal. The challenge to himself had been transferred onto a playing field, and gradually Giacomo permitted me to return the ball to him, giving me the livelier role of a player. Coming close to losing was still a very difficult experience precisely because of the accompanying sense of being overwhelmed or crushed. When it happened that he could not protect himself, a series of violent shots were initiated. It seemed to me that through this play, Giacomo was working through the serious aggression that he had experienced, permitting him to express in play the anger that had been aroused.

One day, during the second session of the week, he took the little tennis ball that he had substituted for the paper one and wrapped it inside a sheet of paper. I thought that he had put the two of us together, and I felt that this gesture, which broadened the play and varied it, was like a fuller restitution of that first intense contact that happened in 'playing horsey'.

His lump of paper, too, had opened up and had a playful heart inside. He shot the double-layered ball to me with his hands, quite hard. This gesture made me think of the delivery of a letter wrapped around a stone. I opened the paper and, pretending to write to him (he had recently learned to write, and I didn't want an overly scholastic effort to interrupt the play), I said, 'I received a letter, but I can't read it', and I threw the ball with the paper over it back to him.

He hid under the table and, scribbling on the paper, he answered, 'I wrote to you in a secret alphabet'.

Again through the mail system that we had invented, I answered, 'I need your help'.

Giacomo: 'I wrote that if you don't learn to save goals, I'll kill you'. Giacomo was placing his impotence in me and thereby expressing the rage that it aroused in him.

Putting myself in his shoes, I wrote, 'I've learned to save a few goals but not all of them'.

He answered, 'Come find me in my lair. Come – if you don't, I'll kill you'.

I threw the paper back to him, having (actually) written, 'Dear Raging Tiger, I'll come at 5:00' (that was the time of our meetings).

Angrily, he threw back my paper on which he had made a correction – 'infuriata' was changed to 'infuriato' – and he added the word 'idiot'.[14]

Immediately, I thought that my words must have caused an increase in his anxiety about suffering a mutilation, but besides this unconscious fantasy, I knew that his parents had greatly emphasized his behaving well in the hospital as the result of his being a boy, and they had frequently spoken to me of his exemplary behaviour during his recovery periods, attributing this capacity to his gender. My involuntary creation of a connection between his anger and being feminine had produced an unacceptable emotional result, because at the same time, it had increased his anxiety and damaged the sense of self-worth that his parents had in their own way provided him with. I tried to remedy the situation by writing to him: 'Dear Tiger [here I used the masculine form of the adjective, accepting his correction even though it was linguistically incorrect], I know you are a boy. Boys are generally better at playing ball games', but this correction did not alleviate his anger. We reached the end of the hour with difficulty because a sense of heaviness hung over us; I was very unhappy about having wounded him, and my direct apologies did not have the effect of a real reparation. The next time Giacomo did not come to his session. I was forced to rethink the episode. How had the idea come to me to write to him 'Dear Raging Tiger'? Though linguistically irreproachable, it now seemed more natural to me to have written to him something like 'Dear Giacomo, at times I make you enraged like a tiger'. The word *tiger* did not in fact have much relationship to the play we were engaged in, except to the word *lair*; I had to admit to myself that, in any case, tiger-lair is certainly not one of the word pairings that sometimes result from cultural automatisms. Certainly, it is also difficult to abandon one's own gender identity in play, so I hypothesized that the raging tiger could be me. Underneath the apparent feeling of controlling the process, one of my problematic experiences, though not openly acted out in our play, had found a way to exist within a word. I did not really feel angry, in fact, but certainly Giacomo's play – at intervals unpredictable and violent – made me, too, experience a vague sense of aggression. And thus, with a leap, a tiger that embodied a manifestation of shared sentiments charged into the room through a linguistic referent. His missing the next session – which occurred not because the boy was oppositional but rather because of a real illness – caused me to question myself about how much my not being fully capable of optimal acceptance and transformation of anxiety and rage might have added to the weakening of his body, contributing to his illness.

When Giacomo returned, he appeared to me to be a little worried. He had had a fever. I, too, had felt unwell in falling prey to feverish thoughts; I could understand.

He showed me how he had lain in bed for the entire day and where his head had really hurt. He was lying down as he explained. 'Why didn't you come see me?' he asked.

I didn't really know what to say. 'I was a little under the weather myself. Last time, I didn't know how to play well with you'.

'Will you come see me the next time I get sick?' Giacomo asked in a calm voice, as though he had already come to terms with his rage at my being there and knowing how to help him.

'Can I come into your lair?' I asked enthusiastically; this was a welcome I had not hoped for.

'If you bring me a present, yes.... Then I'll explain to you where I live'.

I brought a little tiger, wrapped it in a sheet of paper, and gave it to him. He smiled at me and sat upright. The play had begun again.

Elements that can consolidate the capacity to play

This second clinical sequence, which occurred two years after the first one and that thus belongs to a more evolved phase of the analysis with Giacomo, encouraged my reflective return to an analysis of the process in order to explore the ingredients that can indicate a more consolidated capacity to play. At the same time, a perception of their less frequent occurrence can make one aware of a way of functioning that is wearing down slightly.

As I mentioned, Miura's discovery that slanted folds were less wearing than perpendicular ones found a practical application in the folding of a topographical map. How much did my play space and Giacomo's overlap with each other in a way that created the minimal amount of friction possible and analogously that generated new and creative folds? At this point in the analysis, the playing field between Giacomo and me seemed to be defending against the episodes of serious crumpling up that had marked the first year; the climate of the relationship had changed, and the analytic field had expanded to the degree that we had succeeded in exploring it. Let me clarify by saying that the expansion of the field and the ability to remain engaged in play do not in themselves avoid the creation of misunderstandings and enactments, but they do set things up so that these can be repaired much more easily. It is the experience of having creatively produced and maintained the relationship for a long time that metabolizes a large part of the emotional tension inevitably produced in the relationship and that avoids the unconscious acting out of serious fractures.[15]

In the clinical passage under examination, a more consolidated capacity to play permitted Giacomo and me to better master the unpredictability of unconscious emotions and to more easily develop thoughts that could think these emotions.

This better functioning, both conscious and unconscious, made itself tangibly felt in the relationship in the sense of greater mutual trust. "*Confidence in the mother*", writes Winnicott, "*makes an intermediate playground. . . . I call this a playground because play starts here*".[16] Trust can thus be thought of as a specific affective form capable of imprinting onto the analytic situation an efficacious functioning that for Winnicott coincides with the beginning of the capacity to play. Besides being a basic emotion, it is, in my opinion, an emotion that is consolidated when a couple has experienced the joint capacity of being able to creatively repair the most turbulent emotional situations – or, to use Bion's words, to dream them.

In the second clinical passage, I felt a sensation of trust inside myself, a feeling that had a determining weight in allowing me to more rapidly consider my responsibility in what had happened and that had also in part influenced the rediscovery of an emotional attunement after the missed session. From the perspective of the bi-personal field, then, trust seems to be an emotional derivative of the couple's functioning once it has become capable of increasing its tolerance for problematic emotions.

The greater capacity to remain in play was revealed in Giacomo, too, when he crumpled the paper over the tennis ball, inventing a composite object that could contain a turbulent emotion born of the relationship with me. The aspect that struck me intensely and that I want to underscore here was that, on his return, Giacomo knew how to demonstrate to me that he had internalized – in addition to a capacity to work through his emotions autonomously – a new relational competence as well. He knew how to use me in the session for further working through, and at the same time, he knew how to nourish me, in turn, through the gift of an unhoped-for capacity for acceptance. The invitation to go to his home in fact bore witness to Giacomo's new capacity to face his own rage and to work through a feeling that, although to different degrees, we had introduced into the field. His capacity to nourish me restored a sense of reciprocity and consolidated trust about our knowing how to construct and reconstruct the playing field together. The little package with the tiger inside, as I have described, then became the concrete gesture that expressed our joint capacity to contain and work through the hate and other aggressive aspects present in the field.

The folds of and in the setting: the nervous system of a living process

I would like to briefly point out how the setting can also be bent or folded or, vice versa, can be expanded, thanks to the removal of obstructive aspects, within relational play that has been expanded to encompass the child's parents. After two years of therapy, Giacomo's parents had invested in the construction of a new home, and this had given them leave to ask me for a reduction in the frequency of sessions. In a meeting with them, I managed to convince them not to reduce the frequency right away, without excluding the possibility of our doing so after the summer break, hoping that after the summer, it would be possible to maintain the same frequency. I had supported the opportunity to maintain the same frequency of sessions, and I had tried to explore together with the parents the emotional difficulties that for now, however, they could tell me about only through the economic aspect of Giacomo's treatment. When they left the studio, accepting my proposal, I felt satisfied, at any rate. It was in this manner that they began not paying me. I went back to meeting with them, and I tried to listen more closely to their feeling of being exploited somehow – a feeling that I now concretely shared.

In a certain sense, my rigid assumption of the hypothesis that a high frequency of sessions permitted better analytic work had implied an analogously rigid exclusion of their request, creating a situation in which the process apparently continued to function but with a high risk of fracture. I felt alarmed at the concrete possibility of losing Giacomo, and the turbulence of emotions crumpled up my thoughts. How could we produce a playful setting – that is, make it a creative invention that could represent the capacity to take care of and to feel cared for – for all the subjects of this analysis? The explicit dialogue about the emotional difficulties that I had sought in my earlier meeting with the parents had not produced anything other than the risk of making them experience an unfathomable distance from the way in which, in that moment, they were able to communicate their ambivalence to me. I requested an additional meeting in which I decided to ask them in what way I could contribute to the construction of their new home. Knowing that my proposal could not have too concrete a meaning, I imagined it could be located by all of us in that transitional area in which gestures have a mandate of both truth and fiction at the same time. They appeared to reach a solution without being at all disconcerted by my proposal. They suggested a break of one month in which they would not pay me. This savings of time and money, they explained to me, would permit them to choose the finishing touches for their new home. I asked whether they could in exchange be responsible for writing a weekly e-mail to me in which they would describe their play with Giacomo, given that they would be the ones playing with him in my place.

I think that this possibility of choosing the finishing touches of their home, temporarily excluding me, had to do with their desire to feel they were capable of successfully concluding the reconstruction of their real child as well as the one contained in their minds. I thought that perhaps they had felt robbed of their capacity in this sense. I decided to communicate the decision to Giacomo. I felt some apprehension, however, about the effects that this brusque interruption would have on Giacomo, and I also feared that it could be an encouragement of the interruption on my part. But Giacomo's parents kept their word. In fact, the mother wrote to me more often than we had agreed upon. She gave me news of Giacomo in e-mails, emphasizing that the boy did not ask about me and that this could mean he no longer needed the analysis. Through the way this was pointed out, I was able to understand how much fear the mother must have experienced, of being less capable than I was. At the same time, it seemed to me that, through writing, she could legitimize and explicate the rivalry between us that had tended to be negated in our face-to-face meetings. In her letters, the mother told me how she had had occasion to observe Giacomo while he was playing alone in his room. She told me nothing about the play itself, but she assured me of his ability to play alone. I imagined that in this way, the mother was turning upside down the paradigm she had experienced when she had remained in the waiting room during

Giacomo's sessions. I replied to all these letters, trying to accept both the communications about Giacomo and the mother's suffering. In the next to the last letter, in contrast, she described a game that she and Giacomo had played together the previous Sunday. They had constructed a large box in which to store toys in the new house, and then they had transformed the box into a little fort and together they had played war.

I thought that this game had a double function: that of giving testimony to the mother's capacity to construct a container for Giacomo, the defective child whom she had – perhaps for the first time – succeeded in accepting into her heart, and also the possibility of the long internal war that both of them had had to go through. In this same letter, the mother announced the possibility of resuming the treatment; she added, however, in a peremptory way, that Giacomo could come only twice a week. I accepted, and Giacomo resumed analysis, terminating after a further year and a half of treatment.

Despite the difficulty that I think every analyst may have in accepting a reduction in the frequency of sessions, it seemed more acceptable to me to think of this as perhaps the expression of the parents' improved capacity to take care of their child's emotions. My acceptance was also a recognition of that psychic new home that they had been able to construct.

As Petrella[17] suggests, the variation in the setting that I put into practice shifted the question from what I should do or should have done to what I was doing. This question allowed me to grasp that I had folded the setting in a way that wasn't rigid to a type of play that could recreate the shared experience of being cared for – for the parents as well, who were indispensable actors in the child's therapy. The invented way of folding in fact allowed the parents to face the painful feeling of being dispossessed of their competence in caring for their own child.

If play is the first creative format that the child invents to cope with the absence of the maternal body and to recreate the pleasure of early play experienced with the mother,[18] then why not think of the setting as a form of play to be created together with the parents?

Play in the relational field

Winnicott describes play as the reflection of a complex process of the child's psychic maturation in its relationship with the mother. When he writes that psychotherapy consists of the overlap of two areas of play, that of the patient and that of the analyst, he is speaking of the phenomenon of the couple's psychic development while its members work together – a development that Winnicott maintains is so central that it determines the qualitative measure of the very development of the analytic process.

Studying, then, the capacity to play – what it consists of and how it develops – Winnicott made some observations that seem useful to me in order to gain an indirect measurement of the unconscious work that the analyst-patient couple is capable of carrying out and thus to have an indirect measurement of the functioning of the intersubjective contact barrier. I have considered three *"emotional derivatives"* in particular: the sensation of pleasure, that of reciprocity and the development of trust. Winnicott describes the birth of pleasure as the conscious emotional consequence of play based on his observation of nursing. He writes, *"Settled in for a (breast) feed, the baby looks at the mother's face and his or her hand reaches up so that in play the baby is feeding the mother by means of a finger in her mouth"*.[19] Winnicott highlights that play has its roots in a bodily experience accompanied by a feeling of contentment and pleasure tied to the subsiding of hunger. The body, in turn, is the place where an attitude is born that represents the first iteration of the creative experience. It begins in the child through perceptive experiences, tactile and kinaesthetic ones, that permit the birth of fantasies expressed through bodily functioning. These early imaginative iterations, which Gaddini defines as *"fantasies in the body"*,[20] evolve into *"fantasies about the body"*; not only visual experience is capable of functioning as a psychic catalyst. Winnicott, in the comment quoted, describes the moment in which the child, through a particular visual experience, becomes capable of an attitude through which it uses the fantasy of the breast to establish a new way of being in a relationship. Here, the fantasy seems to involve bodies in a way in which they are both distinct and confused at the same time. In Winnicott's description of the moment in which play is born, the child's gesture is not only an imitative one. The imitative experience is a method of familiarization with selfness but is beyond intentionality.[21] In Winnicott's description, the creative use of the finger is a gesture that, beginning with imitation, expresses a capacity to transform an emotional experience into an effective attitude within the relationship, permitting the child to experience an early form of conscious participation – that is, the child moves from a position of its ownness to one of participation. The aspect I would like to emphasize is that Winnicott locates the birth of play at the crossroads of an aesthetic experience with a profound relational resonance, an experience that will be laid down in unconscious memory. The goodness experienced through the consumption of milk merges with the goodness of contemplating the maternal face, and both these elements contribute to generating an intense sensation of pleasure. Winnicott himself uses the word *mutual* to describe this complex feeling of fullness and shared pleasure: "*[There] does not exist a communication between the baby and the mother except insofar as there develops a mutual feeding situation*".[22] Obviously, Winnicott is not misunderstanding the directionality of responsibility for physical and psychic nurturing, but he emphasizes that, when a feeling of reciprocity is achieved, the emotional tonality of the communicative exchange assumes the pleasant quality and effect that are typical of play. Even though Winnicott did not fully develop this idea, when he alludes to reciprocal nourishment, he seems to mean that when a relationship – including the analytic one – is used as a transitional space, both subjects have the opportunity to be nourished, discovering through the other something of the self.[23] In fact, he goes so far as to define the psychoanalytic process as "*a highly specialized form of playing in the service of communication with oneself and others*".[24] To summarize, it seems to me that Winnicott is describing the birth of a conscious and unconscious communicative capacity and emphasizing that this capacity grows through an experience of pleasure and mutuality. Bion describes something similar, even though from a different theoretical perspective, in regard to the unconscious exchange between mother and child. He writes, "*Leaving aside the physical channels of communication, my impression is that her love [the mother's] is expressed by reverie*".[25] The capacity to stabilize a link, L, which is a constructive link and the generator of meaning, is transmitted and taught by the mother to the child through two functions: the capacity to dream the raw emotions that exceed the child's transformative capacity and a sort of interpretation in action, which are the caretaking actions in response to emotional, unconscious entreaties. These actions create an unconscious communicative channel which, together with maternal reverie, cooperates in the construction of the child's mental container. The intersubjective link L and the good functioning of the intrasubjective contact barrier, then, exist in relation to the quantity of a work that two minds in a relationship can carry out. Even though Bion does not specifically cite the conscious emotional consequence of this unconscious functioning, it is possible to imagine that the link L makes itself felt through a pleasurable harmony or the feeling of being in unison.

Both Bion and Winnicott underline the aspect of conscious and unconscious co-construction in the relationship, which is accompanied and at the same time nourished by the sensation of pleasure. If patient and analyst learn to use themselves reciprocally, unconsciously – becoming, as Bion suggests, in one moment the container with the other the contained, and in the next moment trading roles – then they will be able to experience a feeling of truly playing together. In fact, play is perceived as such when each of the participants feels enriched and nourished by the other. When one of the two subjects feels too great of an advantage over the other, a sort of crumpling can be produced, in contrast. An example of this imbalance in my illustrative case was the formulation in the session of psychopathological hypotheses that implicitly tended to attribute the responsibility for what was happening in the field to the patient's difficulty in working through. An indicator of the analytic field's good functioning over a longer term period is the feeling of trust. Trust not only initiates play, as Winnicott indicates, but also grows in a way that is directly proportionate to the couple's capacity to remain engaged in play, repairing the inevitable difficulties. When a sense of trust is missing, the playing field's functioning takes on a rigid aspect, because it is only trust in the capacity of the relationship that permits the making of new hypotheses, new folds in one's own and the other's psychic map, and thus of being creative. The sense of trust was consolidated in my relationship with the child when Giacomo permitted a variation of the setting, perhaps a partial acting out of a certain amount of ambivalence that is always present in the relationship between the child therapist and the child's parents. Trust in the capacity of the relationship's resilience contributed in large part to my being used subjectively by them, permitting me to imagine the construction of their new home as the dream of a costly and compelling expansion of the psychic container.

Notes

1 Benni 1992, p. 35. Reprinted with permission of Giangiacomo Feltrinelli Editore.
2 Baranger and Baranger 1961–62, Bezoari and Ferro 1996, Nissim Momigliano 1992, Ogden 1994.
3 For an overview of Miura's work, see Miura 1994, Nishiyama 2012.
4 Ogden 2004b.
5 Winnicott 1953, 1965b, p. 229 and p. 254.
6 Bion 1962a, 1962b.

7 Ogden 2004b, p. 96.
8 Ogden 1997, p. 893.
9 Ferro 2006.
10 Ferro and Foresti 2008.
11 Winnicott 1971, p. 80. The object not yet repudiated has at not-me phenomenon.
12 Ogden 2004b.
13 Stern et al. 1998.
14 In Italian, tiger is a feminine noun and thus the adjective I used, 'infuriata', had the correct linguistic declination.
15 Ferro 2006, Greenberg 1996, Lachmann and Beebe 1996, Ogden 1988, Stern et al. 1998, Winnicott 1971.
16 Winnicott 1971, p. 47.
17 Petrella 1993, p. 140. The observations far in the time and in the language are similar to Ogden 2007, p. 353.
18 I would say a concept of Winnicott 1971 but underlined by Phillips 1988 in his rethinking to Winnicott's thought.
19 Winnicott 1969, p. 255.
20 Gaddini 1982, p. 568.
21 Stensson 2006.
22 Winnicott 1969, p. 255.
23 Sociology, psychology, psychoanalysis: all these fields of knowledge have a weak theoretical paradigm (as discussed by Kuhn 1962 and Feyerabend 1991). But the use, in the practice and in the therapy of the different 'laws', is giving a new kind of scientific value (Ogden 2001, Winnicott 1971).
24 Winnicott 1971, p. 41.
25 Bion 1962b, p. 35.

Chapter 4

A 'quantum' of truth in a field of lies

The investigation of emotional truth in a child analysis

In a widely publicized article, I read that a group of physicists at the National Institute of Material Physics succeeded in demonstrating, through a complex experiment, a brilliant hypothesis formulated fifty years ago by their colleague, Philip Anderson.[1] In 1958, Anderson, without using experimental trials, conjectured that, beyond a certain level of disorder, a solid could undergo an actual transition to a new phase – for example, from being a conductor it could become an insulator. In chilling a particular type of gas almost to absolute zero, physicists at the Centro Nazionale di Ricerca del Gran Sasso[2] observed that atoms 'feel' the presence of light that modifies the energy. With laser beams aimed in various directions, they succeeded in producing 'structures' of light similar to crystals, and they used special cameras to film the movements of the atoms and to see their extended waves along this entire crystal, as the atoms gradually became localized and enclosed themselves within restricted zones that increased the disorder. In order to trap a quantum particle, as Anderson envisioned, it is enough for there to be disorder. It is as though a rough surface would suffice to trap an animal instead of a walled enclosure, adds the author of the article in an attempt to render this idea intuitively conceivable. It is an idea that, in the author's opinion, is somewhat counter-intuitive, as so often happens with quantum mechanics.

When I read this article, I had just finished reading *A Beam of Intense Darkness*, and its author's ideas stimulated my imagination. Grotstein's intuitions and those of Anderson came together in my mind, and it seems to me – though on an intuitive basis – that the way of picturing disorder proposed in this physics experiment can help me to better explore what happened with a young patient of mine who had a problem of gender identity.

A spatial idea of truth

Before setting out the clinical material from which the idea was generated that built on the intuitions of Grotstein and Anderson, I will try to clarify which of the American psychoanalyst's ideas seemed useful to me in formulating some hypotheses on a particular function of the analytic couple.

Grotstein thinks that the child may be endowed very early on with a function that is capable of attributing an initial personal meaning to the emotional fact that impacts him. *"When O intersects our emotional frontier and makes an impression there of its presence, the initial response is the formation or appearance of an α element (personal)"*.[3] In relation with another mind capable of reverie, α elements can continue their transformative path towards elements of the dream, the contact barrier and memory. In the opposite situation, facts are denied by the mind and degraded into β elements and therefore remain impersonal in a space devoid of meaning. Personalization, then, is initially guided by another mind that enters into contact with that of the child and, since the transformative system depends on a relationship, it is always in a state of precarious equilibrium. Ferro, in his review of Grotstein's book, comments:

> Grotstein seems to adopt towards the beta and alpha elements the same procedure that Bion had used in relation to PS-D; no longer, that is, a linear movement from $\beta \rightarrow \alpha$, but an uninterrupted oscillation $\beta \leftrightarrow \alpha$, without a specific finishing line. This complicates, but also makes more lively, unpredictable, and in this sense also open-ended, the activities of thinking, dreaming and feeling.[4]

Ferro also formulates a very stimulating question: does a transformation (we might add in any direction, $\beta \rightarrow \alpha$) truly exist, or do we ourselves modify our way of perceiving β and α?

Different types of lies

I will discuss the problem of lies and truth in the analytic relationship from the perspective of bi-personal field theory, beginning with Bion's thinking.[5] In this context, I will use the word *lie* not so much to indicate the conscious manipulation of truth but – as Bion indicates – as an aspect of an unconscious process that concerns everyone and that has to do with the difficulty of experiencing emotional truth. Bion himself explicates the vital importance of emotional truth for the development of the mind when he writes, "*Healthy mental growth seems to depend on truth as the living organism depends on food*".[6] For this, the aim of analysis remains fundamentally that of saying something "*relatively truthful*"[7] with respect to emotional truth in a given moment, a truth that the patient will be able to use, consciously and unconsciously, for his own psychological growth.[8] A particularly interesting aspect of Bion's reflections on the relationship between truth and lies is that Bion places the emphasis, from the beginning of his observations, on the importance of the relationship between two minds, and this relational root is what distinguishes psychoanalysis from other scientific disciplines.[9]

Freud had already anticipated the idea of the importance of truth and the push in this direction inscribed in the psyche. He thought that unconscious, repressed desire is in itself a form of lie but maintains a pressure toward the truth. Indeed, Freud writes that the unconscious, "*which is ordinarily our opponent, comes to our help, since it has a natural 'upward drive' and desires nothing better than to press forward across its settled frontiers into the ego and so to consciousness*".[10]

We could say that there is an inclination towards truth and communication in the repressed unconscious.[11] In analysis of a phobia in a five-year-old boy, Freud also lays the basis for the development of the distinction between two categories of lies that will be taken up and clarified by subsequent authors. He describes the fantasies and the "*countless extravagant lies*"[12] of Little Hans about the presence of his little sister, a year before her birth, a form of revenge for the deception perpetrated by his father in this regard. In fact, his father declined to explain the sexual act, instead relating the tale of the stork to his son. Freud places Little Hans's extravagant confabulations in an Oedipal context, as a form of retaliation for having been excluded from the parental couple and from the truth of their sexual relationship. In addition to this observation that allows us to understand how this type of lie may interfere with development in a serious way – an aspect that in my opinion is very interesting – is Freud's impassioned emphasis on the way in which the lie may be a response to a relational problem more than an aspect of anomalous development of the capacity to think and metabolize emotions. In fact,

Freud states that, when the child lies, he is simply imitating the adult who lied to him. In this sense, Freud's emphasis anticipates the idea of the lie's deeply relational origin and the profound damages that it involves.

A certain type of dysfunction in the mind of the caregiver – or, subsequently, in the mind of the analyst – can generate a serious distortion in the process of signification and subjectivization. Thus, we can say that utilization of the lie as a conscious manipulation of reality is a process that pertains to everyone, in particular during development, but it has very different psychic implications in cases in which such manipulation is located at the heart of the relationship charged with helping the child bring forth his own mind from his body. Sometimes the lie can permit the child to place something of his own outside himself and, through the other's reaction, to learn to distinguish his desire from reality.[13] In other cases, actualizing a desired event in fantasy can provide the child with the illusion of enjoying an area of omnipotent control in a real world that often overwhelms him.[14] In yet other circumstances, the lie preserves the defensive mandate of protecting the integrity of development but in a somewhat more problematic way. It can be used to distance the defectiveness that the child thinks is unacceptable for his own internal object, or it can protect a private area of the self in a relationship with an intrusive object. Though signalling the presence of relational aspects that are not optimal, this type of lie continues to contain the hope of an object capable of love,[15] and in this sense, it does not seriously compromise the development of thinking.

These different ways of lying that are more or less disturbing to development can be grouped in the category that Lemma[16] defines as "*self-preservative lying*". In the area of analytic therapy, this type of lie – in which the child consciously manipulates reality – can be considered the re-enactment of a particular aspect of Oedipal conflict newly expressed in the transference. Here, the lie accomplishes a screen function with respect to the emergence of Oedipal wishes or fantasies that in this way can be mastered, at least in part.[17] From the perspective of the bi-personal field, the analyst can consider these lies as the narrative derivative of an emotional situation that can barely be faced but that is shareable and thinkable.[18] I will refer to this type of lie in the last part of my clinical report in order to illustrate a positive development in the therapy.

There is, however, a different type of lie that, although also having a defensive aim, originates from a more pervasive disturbance in the development of the apparatus for thinking thoughts, such that in some cases a clear distinction of the self from the non-self is not permitted. From another theoretical perspective in comparison to Bion, O'Shaughnessy,[19] in an article titled 'Can a liar be psychoanalysed?', reflects on the perversity of the disturbance of those patients who habitually lie.

She writes, "*The fundamental problem of the habitual liar . . . is primitive, and involves the truth and falsity of his objects – their genuineness or deceitfulness*". O'Shaughnessy thinks that this type of person may communicate, in a distorted form, an identification with a lying object. An omnipotent object that intrudes and controls the self dominates the internal world of these patients. The lie is thus used in these cases to maintain an unconscious tie and at the same time to separate from the object; it accomplishes the task of creating a border between self and other in the absence of a true paternal triangulation.

Various authors besides Bion, then, have tried to distinguish different ways in which a patient can fail to speak the truth and the implications that these various modalities have on the development of thinking and of the relationship, including the analytic one. Bion makes a distinction between two different types of psyche phenomena in which one cannot speak the truth, introducing a semantic distinction between a falsehood and a lie. Utilizing the instrument of the grid, Bion theorizes that the first type of lie is located in category 6 (action), having the aim of provoking an emotional upheaval: evocative, provocative, accusatory. The lies of the second type are by contrast positioned as belonging to category 2 and are used to maintain a barrier against an emotional upheaval felt as catastrophic.[20] In this second meaning, the lie "*has its counterpart in the domain of being; it is possible to be a lie and being so precludes at-one-meet in O*".[21] Following this Kantian hypothesis, Bion theorizes that the truth does not need a thinker, but the lie, in order to exist, must have someone who gives it a meaning through his own thoughts. When O (the truth that does not belong to the human system) collides with the individual's personality and begins to promote a transformation, the subject feels inhabited by a strong sense of persecution, characteristic of the paranoid-schizoid position. Bion maintains that the elaboration of these experiences can give rise to the possibility of making the subject evolve towards a state of greater mental health, capable of transforming the parasitic tie that exists between the thinker and the lie. Bion does not formulate further hypotheses on how this transformation can take place within the analytic setting.

Following the theoretical expansion of Bion's thought that Grotstein and Ferro propose, I have tried to develop a hypothesis about how this second type of lie can signal not only an injury to the subject's apparatus for thinking thoughts but also a certain degree of disorder in the analytic setting at a crucial and early point in the transformative process of attributing personal meaning to a primitive α element. In attempting a change in the point of observation, then, as suggested by the revealing hypothesis derived from quantum mechanics, I hypothesize that, in the analytic relationship, an incident of acting out that derives from falsification of emotional truth can be seen in a paradoxical way as the powerful activator of a process aimed at reinstating the truth.

A 'field' of lies

In the sphere of field theory, one could reformulate the distinction between the two types of lies as follows: if a mind is not capable of tolerating the emotional truth of a primitive α element, then it will introduce into the field a degree of disorder that can influence the developmental process of a primitive α element of the subject with whom it is in a relationship, creating the possibility that it may move toward being a β element. This perspective accentuates the analyst's responsibility with respect to the events that reveal themselves in the field and imagines emotional truth as a spatial, ordered element and as co-constructed by the relationship.

Thus, in trying to respond to Ferro's stimulus, I imagined the space of the analytic third,[22] the space where unconscious elements of both members of the couple are deposited and enter into contact, as a sort of crystal that is criss-crossed by beams of light. In the psychoanalytic process, the beams of light originate inside each of the subjects, with an early attribution of a personal emotional meaning to the sensations produced by the environment and the interaction. The product of this early transformative, intrasubjective operation gives rise to primitive α elements. Since the development of these primitive α elements is influenced by the presence of another mind in relation with the first, one that is capable of reverie and of influencing further transformations in the direction of the dream, the metaphorical rays of light – made up of transformative sequences – must cross the space of the analytic third. If everything proceeds without difficulty, then the area of the third results in the spatial model imagined as a neat and orderly crystal. When a primitive α element's trajectory does not extend to the possibility of evolving in the space of the third, it can often be – like the wave of electrons described by Anderson – reflected by impurities; it interferes with itself and, from a broad extension, ends up concentrated completely in a restricted zone of the crystal. From being a conductor, a zone of the field becomes disordered and is transformed into an insulator, blocking further transformations. Primitive α elements, joined together, are revealed in the field as 'forms' of distortion of emotional truth. I have imagined that a certain type of lie could be a clinical example of an α element blocked in the early phase of development towards shared meaning and a useful element with which to investigate which type and degree of disorder in the field might be blocking this development. To put it in another way, some types of lies can be imagined as the falling of a primitive α element incapable of further evolution due to some emotional fact that is condensed in the field (see Figure 4.1).

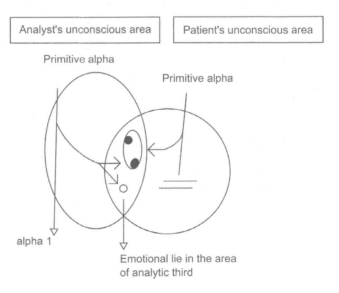

Figure 4.1 Map of α elements incapable to evolve

An early truth entrapped in the body and in family history

Alessandro is a nine-year-old boy who began analysis at the age of six because, after having tried in all possible ways to convince his parents that he was a girl but still unable to obtain their approval, he had decided to turn to God. Every night, he prayed to be able to wake up the next day and see that his dream had finally come true.

Alessandro's father told me that, in his heart, he had already accepted his son's homosexuality; he consulted me to avoid the child's becoming a transvestite, a category of humanity that was intolerable to him. Alessandro's mother, by contrast, was much more aware that something abnormal had happened in the course of his development, and she had great faith in the reversibility of a homosexuality that seemed to her more a sign of something than a real identity.

In listening to the family history, I was able to formulate an initial hypothesis about the genesis of Alessandro's difficulty in correctly identifying himself with his own sexual gender. Within the family, Alessandro's father contained his psychological difficulties through an important obsessive defence that had been constructed to cope with a significant traumatic aspect of his life. As he told it, this was a domestic accident suffered by a childhood friend of his. Because of her parents' negligence, this little girl had overturned a pan of boiling water onto herself, sustaining serious burns all over her body. She had survived, but the intensity of her burns had produced scars that disfigured her for life. This tale might be considered as the best possible narration of the traumatic impact the father had suffered in early adolescence when, following the loss of his own father, his mother had substituted an intolerable turnover of men in his place, to the point of actual prostitution.

Alessandro's father had in some ways repaired this wound with a scar that, as he suggested in his account, continued to disfigure his life, preventing his psychic skin from being sufficiently elastic. His friend's burn accident had been useful for his psychic survival, permitting the projection of an intolerable truth – and especially of intolerable feelings of hatred towards his mother.[23] In his educative relationship with Alessandro, the father's difficulties were evidenced by his demanding an unsustainable orderliness and discipline of the child, accompanied by regret that Alessandro was not as calm and orderly as he imagined little girls were. Deep down in this desire, there was probably a hidden, unconscious wish to change the gender identity of his son, who re-enacted as a male the drama of rivalry with the wife-mother. An additional hypothesis – in regard to the father's declared hatred of transvestites – might have been his unconscious desire for fusion of the two sexual genders into one person, a fusion that radically and magically eliminated the pain of separation and traumatic distancing from his mother.

These aspects and others unknown to me must have contributed to Alessandro's difficulty in accepting his father as a model with whom to identify. The continual manifest conflictuality between father and son hid the father's unconscious conflictuality, which came to fruition in the abusive context illustrated earlier.[24] In a certain sense, childhood sexuality can always be considered to be moulded in the child by the parents' personality structure, meanings and fantasies, almost to the point of our being able to consider it an "*alien internal entity*".[25] But, in considering the paternal problem, one can state that, since birth, Alessandro had suffered from unconscious paternal fantasies and had fallen into the deceitfulness of his own identity, meaning the pressure to adhere to an unconscious, resolutely denied arrangement that his father imposed on him. Alessandro's desire to be a girl also contained the desire to be like his mother and to survive psychically, negating separation and gender difference. The environment in which Alessandro had been immersed virtually prevented the development of a healthy representative capacity, and this factor revealed itself in a systematic distortion of reality, a spectrum of lies of various types. His parents exchanged the frequent lies of Alessandro in a dangerously delinquent tendency; so, as Winnicott suggests,[26] they deprived their child of his creativity, forcing him into a reality of expedience.

Transformation of the field from conductor (of transformations) to insulator

Through a clinical vignette, I will illustrate how the phenomenon of distorted emotional truth was demonstrated in a session with regard to the topic of sexuality. This distortion – which involved me and not the family – pushed me to try to understand what type and degree of disorder might be capable of producing a drastic change in the flow of transformations that continually happen in every subject involved in the analytic field and among these subjects in order to transform β elements into α ones.

In the first session after summer vacation, five months since the beginning of an analytic therapy of three sessions per week, Alessandro brought me a gift: a little wooden statue representing a couple in the act of kissing each other on the mouth. I commented with a statement that, once voiced, astonished even me: 'It is a wet kiss, between grown-ups'. The adjective *wet* came to my mind, perhaps, because the patient's mother had earlier told me by phone that, during the summer, Alessandro's enuresis had greatly intensified. I thought that the absence of analysis had induced him more actively to seek maternal care as a substitute for an interrupted positive experience. A second association that immediately came to my mind was a line in the famous movie *Rain Man*. In a memorable scene, Dustin Hoffman, who plays the part of a man affected by autism, uses the lone adjective *wet* to describe the incredible experience of a kiss with his brother's beautiful fiancée. In my comment, then, there was an implicit description of an emotional incontinence together with a defence of the autistic type. At the conscious level, I felt a sense of unpleasant forcefulness, which I had experienced in the preceding months as well, due to the way with which Alessandro tried to obtain care for himself and closeness. In après-coup I understood that, just as Alessandro's father had produced a wet dream from inappropriately and precociously sexualized context, I, too, had dreamed something distant from the child's emotional need at that moment. The adjective *wet* did not link up with the analytic situation, and in this sense, it was a marker of my difficulty in involving myself in the emotional process at hand – and in going beyond the sensation and the overly objective description, almost autistic, of an encounter.

Alessandro, in contrast, did not seem surprised by my comment and added with a certain malice: 'Do you know that my friend Giulia is always kissing me like this?' Thinking that he had been led to speak to me about his friend Giulia because I had denied the pleasure of affectionate and accepting contact, I said to him, 'I, too, am happy with your gift and also that you've come back'. The conscious intention was that of correcting what had appeared to me as my having functioned unsatisfactorily, while on a deeper level, I had caused the sensation of sexual excitation in myself to disappear, and I had ended up by saying something emotionally incomplete and different from what I had sincerely felt. In addition, Giulia was a character in the field who embodied the desire of how Alessandro wanted to be treated, but this character was positioned in my mind as a rival who was more capable than I was. I myself, in a certain sense, had ended up creating 'confusion' between the generations, putting a little girl in the place of a rival, something that signalled the activation of childishness or perhaps a blind spot in my mind.[27]

In the next quarter of an hour, while the session seemed to stagnate in a joyless atmosphere, I returned in my mind to the first lie that I had a memory of telling. I was about the same age as Alessandro when one day I was given a snack of bread smeared with orange marmalade. That type of bitter flavour did not appeal to me, and it disappointed the expectation of sweetness for which I had prepared myself; as soon as I was alone, I threw the whole thing over the balcony. The speed with which I had finished eating generated surprise and, when asked about the goodness of the snack, I put forth exaggerated praise of it. I clearly remembered the pride with which I felt I had resolved the problem, but at the time, I was afraid that someone, hit by the flying sticky object, might come up and complain. Only many years later could I hypothesize about the meaning of the bitterness that I had wanted to throw far away. That memory had the effect of making me feel again, and intensely so, the necessity for a child to be faithful to what the person on whom he is affectively dependent expects from him, avoiding any recognition of the existence of his own emotions when they are perceived as too dangerous for the relationship. In order to be able to pass from faith in the other to faith in one's self, and thus to be able to speak the emotional truth that upholds the factual truth, it is necessary that one develop a consciousness of the self, one that is acquired slowly through the relationship with another mind capable of dreaming the nightmare of a too-painful distancing. The fact of having lied to Alessandro thus seemed to me to be of some importance because, in transferring the problem onto myself, I was forced to not behave in the defensive way of assigning the problem only to Alessandro. That Alessandro could be having difficulty tolerating the bitterness of the summer break and the sense of exclusion that it had involved, hiding his rage in the lie of an exaggerated love for me, was a hypothesis that seemed to me only a partial description of what had happened, a too unilateral one.

This kind of hypothesis could have been appropriate to the description of an Oedipal-type relationship, while what Alessandro and I were experiencing was emotionally positioned in a much earlier phase of development. Here, the borders between self and non-self proved to be much more vague, the emotions of a paranoid-schizoid type, and the defences put into place against this type of anxiety oscillated between reactions of extreme withdrawal, splitting and violent expulsion, as emerged in my childhood memory and as would prove to be even more clear in the following session.[28] At the end of this session, I was capable only of grasping, as Davies[29] indicated, that Alessandro was again looking for intimacy through a form of proto-eroticism, which was the deformed expression of an unconscious experience of violent psychological penetration. To this situation re-enacted in the transference, I had answered with a form of reactive rigidity to the sense of a violation of borders and with an absolutely unconscious emotional lie. I understood that Bion's statement – that the lie permits one to protect oneself from painful change – was true not only for the patient but also for me. In his words:

> *The emotional upheaval against which the lie is mobilized is identical with catastrophic changes, [so that] it becomes easier to understand why investigation uncovers an ambiguous position which is capable of arousing strong feelings. Their strength derives from risk of change in the psyche.*[30]

The need for closeness that in some measure my mind had picked up, together with a disturbing emotion of forcefulness, had then been intercepted immediately afterward by Giulia's entry into the field, with the retinue of sensations of my inadequacy and rivalry towards a little girl; all that was condensed into a feeling of confusion more than into real thoughts.

Using the model of hypothetical maturation of α elements as an event dependent on an unconscious relationship in the area of the third, the incapacity to experience painful emotions – on both Alessandro's part and mine – had blocked the development of a primitive α element. The emotional lie I had told – that is, that I was happy about his return – had landed in the relational field like a primitive, degraded α element, which manifested itself by involving both our minds in a sticky incapacity to go forward – a bitter marmalade, not at all nutritious for the developmental process of thinking. I wish to make clear that what I said was not a conscious falsification of reality, and thus a lie aimed at affectively approaching Alessandro, because part of me really did experience pleasure at seeing him again. The problematic aspect was the defensive use I had made of that sentiment to elude other, more painful sensations in a way that was quite symmetrical with Alessandro. I had unconsciously removed myself from the evolution of a primitive α element – that is, from his subjectivization that in this case was very painful for me.

In the next session, Alessandro noticed the new statuette that I had placed on a bookshelf together with some games. Rummaging in a box of puppets while talking to himself, he searched for a potential make-believe story in the compendium of fairy tales that his mother read to him at night. 'The dancer and . . . the little soldier', he said to me, beaming. Then he added under his voice, winking at me, 'They love each other'. His little statue was perfect for better explaining to me the concept of loving each other. At a certain point, completely unpredictably, the little statue suddenly hit me violently. I lifted my gaze and saw his triumphant expression as he said, 'The dancer just wanted to do a pirouette!' It was clear that the idea of the pirouette was a falsification of his desire to hit me. It was evident that, through negation of what he had done, Alessandro tried to communicate what he wanted to repress in a negative form.[31] But in saying that, he demonstrated, from a psychic point of view, that in this predicament he was capable of enacting a separation and thus of beginning to distinguish the self from the hated object. The minutes passed in an eternity in which I felt hurt, angry and also responsible for not having predicted what would happen. When I felt calm enough, I made my way with difficulty along the path of emotional truth, which I had laboriously come into initial contact with through assigning value to the images that had arisen in my mind: that of the movie *Rain Man*, which had permitted me to hypothesize how I was assuming a seriously defensive attitude towards Alessandro, and that of my childhood memory, which had permitted me to come into contact with a pain that was then unthinkable and from which I had tried very concretely to liberate myself. The difficulty lay especially in the fact that there were emotional aspects in me that had not reached the possibility of evolving and of assuming an initial outline of meaning. Rivality towards the character of Giulia had put me in contact with a primitive, serious form of ambivalence. This was not a matter of admitting to myself a normal form of ambivalence towards the patient himself but of professing an emotional truth whose psychic danger a part of me felt was still alive. 'We both felt the desire to throw ourselves away', I said to him. Alessandro's episode of acting out in the moment in which he had hurled the statuette at me took the form of an actual β element. But it had landed in the field due to my difficulty in separating the primitive α elements belonging to both of us that had been condensed in the area of the analytic third in the preceding session. Their transformation into more mature α elements had been intercepted by an obstacle that the analytic frame had permitted us to come into contact with but not yet to fully understand and transform.

The crystal made of light: a device for understanding the β↔α oscillation

The process of thinking begins with the projective identification of *"thoughts (emotions) without a thinker"*,[32] those of the little child inside the maternal mind that functions as a container. The mother, through her reverie and her α function, transforms these primitive elements into thoughts, feelings, dream thoughts and memories. As soon as the child reaches sufficient maturation of his α function, he begins to think on his own, projecting inside his own internal container the primitive elements of thought. In a short time, the subject who projects, and the subject inside of whom the contents are projected, constitute two separate systems that self-activate, but the interpersonal process is bidirectional very early on – such that one can define the unconscious exchange between the subjects as projective trans-identification.[33] In this developmental model of thinking, the two subjects in the relationship project emotions from one to the other and are reciprocally used to elaborate them. The idea of being able to use the other's reverie to achieve a leap towards growth is one of Bion's most fascinating ideas. The other's reverie permits one to go beyond one's own possibilities or capacities to cope with more painful emotions. In fact, if we could do this only through our capacity for thinking, then we would find ourselves trapped in a sort of vicious cycle: we would be able to contain emotions up to the point at which we are capable of thinking of them, and, vice versa, we would be able to think of them only to the degree to which we are capable of containing them.[34]

In the interaction with Alessandro, it had happened that the attribution of a personal, painful meaning to a primitive α element had provoked a gathering of both the patient's primitive α elements and the analyst's, since – even though I had felt a certain type of pain – I was not able to suffer it and so *"to discover it"*.³⁵ The interpretation that followed could not accompany the child, then, in grasping the emotional truth, in that it contained within itself a certain degree of falsification. The incapacity to contact the emotional truth of both had thus produced disorder in the field of the third, and subsequently also in the field of play that is the relational consequence of an orderly emotional field, and one able to function as a conductor of emotions in order to permit development. Orderly, obviously, does not mean devoid of negative feelings or of upsets but capable of moving forward, in the literal sense of moving together towards α. The evolution of the analytic process, which is emotionally dependent on a climate of pleasure and on the reciprocal feeling that supports it, had been seriously disturbed. In the field of play, then, the gathering of primitive α elements from both of us had been manifested through the falsification of Alessandro's desire to hit me; at this point in the process, the lie took the form of acting out.

However, what appeared to be a decline in the capacity to think actually contained the capacity to be reciprocally used and therefore the seed of further transformations. My childhood memory had been an early reverie on the process taking place in the analytic field³⁶ – an initial indication, barely conscious, that my interpretation appeared to be curative but in fact hid my annoyance and consequently an affective distancing. Alessandro had correctly perceived something that he had considered disappointing. Since the priority in terms of psychic existence is that of not losing relational contact, Alessandro, as a weaker subject, had been pushed to draw on a similar mode of functioning through a falsification of his own emotional truth. His gesture of acting out, which derived from this and which to all intents and purposes could be seen as a β element in the relational field, could also be considered as a primitive α element in the field of the third.³⁷

The elaboration in action of the bi-personal emotional disorder that Alessandro had succeeded in producing, from a certain point of view, had opened up for the analyst the possibility of gaining access through bodily and psychic pain and had contributed considerably to the separation of the two primitive α elements. Thus, a β element brought into the field of the analytic third can also constitute an expanding element of the capacity to think for both members of the couple, as long as the couple is emotionally engaged in the relationship, and as long as the analyst succeeds in describing and understanding the emotional factors that have produced a paralysis in the transformative process. In this sense, β and α can find themselves in oscillation between each other, and their definition can sometimes depend on the point of view of the person considering those elements (see Figure 4.2).

Bion himself, in *Elements of Psychoanalysis*, deconstructed the β-α opposition, writing:

> *The scattered β elements can be considered (insofar as they require the ♀ a rudimentary container prototype, a container with non-rigid structure ... The dispersion of β elements presents analogies with the preconception that must be paired with an implementation in order to produce a conception.*[38]

In this quotation, Bion referred in a particular way to the early phases of development in which β elements would behave like a primitive form of container that anticipates the generative encounter of a container – contained meaning through a mimetic adherence to the shape or to the physical characteristics of the object.

I hypothesize that, in the analytic third, the encounter between the β elements of both members of the couple can behave like a primitive form of container and that the mimetic properties of the β elements create an initial sense of 'moving along', inseparable from an immediate interaction. In this sense, they produce a dispersive movement that makes possible the gradual maturation of primitive α elements. By contrast, their

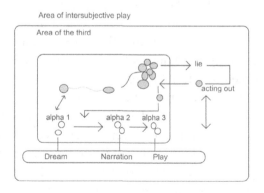

Figure 4.2 Map of transformation of a β element into an α one

condensation would produce a β element incapable of evolving and destined to be evacuated. The condensation can be understood as an incapacity to experience an emotion (an emotional lie) due to an interference produced by the mind of the early caregiver and then by the analyst.

The emotional lie would have an important role in generating this second type of evolution. According to this hypothesis, the β-α evolution would be much less rigidly determined, but the β and α elements would be in a much more dynamic movement between themselves – and also, as Ferro[39] suggested, the very definition of some phenomena in the field, as β or α elements would turn out to be more dependent on the point of observation.

Lies in transformation in the direction of the dream, the narration, the play

In Alessandro's analysis, after the events to which I have referred in detail – in which emotional misunderstanding was expressed at a level not easy to master – the problem of lying continued to be present in the relationship and had the possibility of being further metabolized through subsequent transformations, to the point of generating lies of the self-preservative type.

Just before the following year's Christmas break, but in a situation of prolonged separation analogous to the preceding one, at the end of a session, Alessandro ran into the waiting room where his mother was. He sat himself down sideways on a chair and some little objects fell out of his pocket and onto the floor. He had taken them from my office without my having noticed. His mother did not recognize them as his own playthings, and she asked Alessandro where they had come from; he answered that a schoolmate had given them to him. I again found myself – as though on a level of greater awareness – in the difficult situation of managing the truth. Now Alessandro was lying out of necessity. The beginning of the vacation had pushed him to take possession of the analysis – not yet an internalized frame – in the form of little toy human figures. This manipulation of the truth could be considered a symptom of hope[40] because, in re-establishing omnipotent control over me, Alessandro could enjoy the illusion of not losing me. I told him that it was very important to feel that, during the break, he could continue to play with his friends, and I included myself in this category without specifically naming myself. I turned my gaze to his mother, looking for her agreement. I had again lied, or rather both of us had lied, yet our lies had reached a certain level of manoeuvring in triangulation with the mother, who was responsible to both of us for a greater degree of truth. She agreed to 'look the other way', a precondition for the development of the game.

The following day, during the next to last session before the break – as children surprisingly know how to do – Alessandro was able to make another leap on his own in the direction of further growth. In our play, while I was the mom and he was the dad, he picked up a toy telephone to order a pizza. Pretending to give an order, he turned to me and asked, 'You, love, what do you want?' He waited a moment, then added with an expression of congenial complicity, 'Notice that I call you "love" only because we're playing!' Now we were really playing, and love could reside in a playful little lie that was now weaving between us as reciprocal, genuine pleasure in playing together.

The process of very painful subjectivization of a primitive α element – which had begun some months earlier through our both remaining trapped in the area of the third – had reached one of its evolutionary outcomes. Expressing it in more classical terms, we could say that the underlying relationship in this last clinical fragment was of an openly Oedipal type. Alessandro was capable of clearly distinguishing the self from the object of desire, and the brief fright experienced after the involuntary manifestation of his desire indicated the good functioning of his superego. Thinking could produce real playing, which bore witness to his having reached a more symbolic capacity. But with respect to this reading that is more centred on the patient's development, it just so happens that Alessandro had opened up for me – and, paradoxically, through acting out – the possibility of escaping from the emotional entrapment into which I had fallen and of permitting the development of a primitive α element of mine as well.

Grasping emotional truth

With Alessandro, I experienced a spectrum of falsifications that evolved into my particular way of seeing during the course of the therapy. Initially, I think that his wanting to be a little girl, trying to construct a false gender identity for himself with the aim of rediscovering affective closeness, might have derived from the traumatic distortion in his relationship with his parents. His way of searching for this closeness produced a troubling feeling, in his parents and in me, as though of something out of place. During the analysis, I saw this early 'falseness' with respect to his sexual gender transform itself into a series of lies of various kinds, and, parallel to the development of these lies, Alessandro reacquired the freedom to be himself, as though his creative part could emerge from the superficiality that entrapped it.

In order to promote transformations in therapy with this child, an imaginative model was useful to me, one that permitted me to understand how the interaction of our minds produced a thickening or a thinning of the emotional material that was made visible within a spectrum of lies, as though the lie were a condensed emotion in the zone of a metaphorical relational crystal. When the unconscious lie was produced in an early stage of the transformation of a β element into an α one, it caused a reversal of the flood of transformation and provoked an emotional plummeting in the area of the analytic third, very difficult to transform. Just as Anderson hypothesized for electrons, emotions that weave the outline of the relationship had been suddenly condensed into a place in the field, transforming the field itself from conductor to insulator. The analyst's missed contribution in the process of subjectivization seems to have played a key role in producing not only the emotional condensation and so the regression of a primitive α element toward a β element but also the fall of that β-β aggregate in the intersubjective field in the form of acting out. The surprising aspect for me was that this 'solid' state could have been newly transformed into a conductor of emotions precisely through the incident of acting out. Such an incident can awaken the analyst's mind from a certain sluggishness, pushing her towards the necessity of posing further questions to herself that test the process, but it can especially indicate the early dysfunction of the analytic setting precisely in an area of early transformation – that of subjectivization of a primitive α element. In addition, it seemed to me that the model drawing on quantum physics has permitted me to grasp with more clarity that the definition of a β or an α element does not represent a factual description but rather describes an oscillating phenomenon in the field of the third, and that such a description turns out to be dependent on the point of observation in which the analyst places himself.

Notes

1 The article to which I refer appeared in the weekly insert on culture in the Italian daily newspaper *Il Sole-24 Ore* (8 June 2008). In 1977, P. W. Anderson was awarded the Nobel Prize in physics for his investigations into the electronic structure of magnetic and disordered systems.
2 This is Italy's most prestigious research centre for atomic studies.
3 Grotstein 2007, p. 61.

4 Ferro 2008a, p. 873.
5 Baranger and Baranger 1961–62, Grotstein 2004b, Ogden 2003.
6 Bion 1965, p. 38.
7 Bion 1982, p. 8.
8 Ogden 2004a, p. 292.
9 Bion 1970, pp. 53–54. A science of relationships has yet to be established, and one would look to find some discipline analogous to mathematics to represent the relationship of one element in the structure of the psychic personality with another. It is possible to argue that mathematical formulations can be fully appreciated because there is always some more concrete background to which they can be seen to relate, even though that background may itself be only mathematical.
10 Freud 1938, p. 179.
11 Pellizzari 2010.
12 Freud 1909, p. 129.
13 Fonagy and Target 1996. For the relationship between psychic development and emotional landscape, see also Halpert 2000.
14 Forrester 1997. Although the writing is not mainly a psychoanalytic study.
15 Alvarez 1992. See in particular chapter 14.
16 Lemma 2005, p. 738.
17 Weinshel 1979. In 2009, Goisis tried to research the spectrum between a normal lie and a pathological one in adolescence. Wilkinson and Hough 1996 observed that the behaviour of the analyst should be different with lies that "*can function as narrative truth*".
18 Ferro 1994, Hanly 1990, Spence 1982.
19 O'Shaughnessy 1990, p. 187.
20 Bion 1963, Riolo 1981.
21 Bion 1970, p. 104.
22 As defined in Ogden 1994.
23 Billow 2004 applies the Bionian function container-contained to a case of a falsifying adolescent. See also Wilkinson and Hough 1996.
24 An open issue remains the relation of gender identity and same-sex parents. See Diamond 1997, Davies and Eagle 2013.
25 Laplanche 1976, p. 48.
26 Winnicott 1984.
27 Guignard 1997.
28 Holder 1982.
29 Davies 2001.
30 Bion 1970, p. 99.
31 Freud 1925.
32 Bion 1970, p. 104.
33 Grotstein 2005, p. 1055.
34 Godbout 2004.
35 Bion 1970, p. 9.
36 Ogden 2007.
37 Bion 1962b.
38 Bion 1963, pp. 54–55.
39 Ferro 2008a.
40 Winnicott 1984.

Chapter 5

The anteroom

A camera obscura for grasping aspects that are invisible in the classical setting

Every day, the sound of my office doorbell ushers in a somewhat repetitive sequence: the patient arrives, we shake hands, cross the anteroom[1] and then go into the consulting room. After the session, the route is more or less the same, but the other way round. At the beginning of a session, it is not unusual for me consciously to register sense data from the patient on his[2] way in, such as, for example, the sound of footsteps on the stairs or the use of the elevator or how the patient's eyes and my own meet or avoid each other – thus triggering fantasies or hypothetical attributions of meaning in me. At the end of the session, on the other hand, I feel that my mind is relaxing and relinquishing the task of continuing to pay active attention to the other party in a state of tension. I am, as it were, allowing myself a short break in which to go back inside myself, and as soon as the patient is on the threshold of the consulting room, whereas I was previously profoundly mingled with him in empathy, I am already enjoying a feeling akin to the pleasure of being "*alone in the presence of someone*".[3] As a consequence of these various states of mind, while the situation in the anteroom before the analytic session always arouses my curiosity, so to speak, what occurs in this architectural and mental space at the end of the session has first and foremost the effect of surprising me. Thus, the anteroom is not only the environment that precedes the consulting room but also a place in the mind where I experience different states of being with the patient. While attuned to these initial impressions, I noticed an architectural detail that had always been before my eyes although I had never paid conscious attention to it or assigned it a specific meaning. Whereas the room in which I practise psychoanalysis is flooded with sunshine and light for most of the day, the anteroom is a relatively dark space, lit only indirectly or artificially. The anteroom (anticamera) then appeared to me as a kind of camera obscura that could project wrong-way-round images of my patients or myself onto the wall. Aside from the reversal of the image, which is a visual reflection of surprise as the experiential consequence of an unusual perspective, this optical device gives rise to other visual effects, which have been used by various painters since the sixteenth century.[4]

In a camera obscura, the image is slightly flattened and hence brought closer and rendered more visible because projection through the pinhole cancels out the effect of the focal distance. Another advantage is that it facilitates the representation of even a very extensive landscape within a confined space, and, by restricting the natural light, allows the perception of subtle shades of colour. To summarize, the image observable in a camera obscura is contained within more readily representable dimensions, has less well-defined contours, which therefore appear somewhat more fluid, and its tonal gradation is more strongly emphasized.

Transposed to the analytic situation, this optical phenomenon has helped me to imagine the architectural space of the anteroom as a place in the mind that can modify the focal distance between the patient and myself, thus changing the way in which we relate to each other. This chapter is an attempt to describe some of these relational events and to arrive at hypotheses about the mind at work in a transitional area between being inside and being outside the analytic situation, in which the patient's contribution has made unexplored areas of the relationship representable. Furthermore, living images have arisen within the space of the anteroom, entering the mind from a different angle and hence throwing light on certain limiting aspects of the exploration of the analytic field undertaken by the patient and myself in the consulting room.

The camera obscura and the anteroom in relation to the setting

For a long time, the setting was regarded as an aspect not forming part of the actual process of analysis, a kind of external frame defining the space and time of the analytic encounter; however, it has gradually come to be seen in analytic theory as playing a more active, more intimate part in the process itself. Qualitative aspects such as the rhythm of the sessions and the stability of location have been identified as, in effect, repeating the primary function of maternal holding in the analytic process. Understood in this way, the setting guarantees a sense of security that allows the patient to regress – that is, to discover something of his own personality and his most archaic mode of relating.[5] The setting, in its holding function, affords protection from traumatic discontinuity and therefore contributes actively to the recreation of a relational situation that can facilitate psychic development.

Spatio-temporal discontinuity, on the other hand, may be conducive to the emergence of psychotic elements of the personality, related to archaic aspects such as the autistic-contiguous position or, more simply, to primary fusional needs.[6]

Again, whereas the setting was originally seen as a device favourable to the patient's psychic transformation, it is now widely regarded as capable of conditioning the minds of both analyst and patient at work. Thus, the setting has increasingly come to be seen as a mental function more intimately connected with the process.[7] In field theory, the setting can indeed be regarded less as a factor in the initiation of the analytic relationship and more as an element of psychoanalysis that is generated by the relationship itself.[8] For in terms of the relationship seen from within, it is the α elements that the couple can generate which come together to produce an intersubjective contact barrier in a state of constant transformation, whose permeability determines the capacity of both analytic subjects to dream. From this perspective, the setting is no longer the external spatio-temporal frame that guarantees the process but the external counterpart of the intersubjective contact barrier.

Certain interactions that take place outside the consulting room but in mental contiguity with it can therefore justifiably be deemed phenomena of the analytic field and hence phenomena that fall within the definition of the setting in a wider sense of the word. For this reason, I shall consider certain interactions in the anteroom as something that take place in a specific architectural space as well as use the dimension of space – a space that permits the observation of elements that are not fully perceptible in the consulting room – to explore an area of the mind in the process of relating.

From this point of view, the concrete experience of the camera obscura has helped me to understand how a given setting can guide my perception towards details neglected in the natural environment and how this optical device can facilitate their representation. In the anteroom, one is not on the analytic stage, but one's mental disposition preserves a degree of immersion in the dark that excludes external reality. This, then, is a transitional area between inside and outside, in which certain details invisible in the light become more obvious by virtue of the change of mental setting. In seeking to focus on the variations in one's mental state in the anteroom, I can say that, having exited the consulting room, I feel as if I am emerging from a state of intense, vivid involvement in emotions, achieved by way of relative separation from my thoughts. However, this state of deep immersion in the emotions of the field also entails a relatively non-critical espousal of the mass of earlier thoughts deposited in the setting and in the explicit or implicit theory whereby each analyst attempts to master the chaotic tangle of emotions.[9] Outside the consulting room, softening of the stabilizing foundation of theories affords access to emotions and facts allowing involvement from a different perspective. This, I believe, is why I have several times had the experience in the anteroom of being surprised by the other or of surprising myself in the presence of the other.[10] On the basis of the clinical situations reported next, I shall attempt to explore in particular the role of the setting – or rather, how the shared mental space can determine what we are able to apprehend, represent and dream together.

Alice: the fluid, wrong-way-round image

Alice is a twelve-year-old girl suffering from selective mutism; during her therapy sessions, her eyes are fixed for the entire hour on the floor, and she is unable even to whisper a single word. Three years have passed since we first met, and an enormous number of attempts have been made to build a relational bridge without words.

One day, at the street door as she leaves, I see her eyes lift up from the ground and hear her exchange a few words with her mother, who has come to collect her. I have already said goodbye to her and followed her into the anteroom after a brief delay so that Alice probably feels that she is already outside and, like myself, no longer feels the anxiety generated by the presence of the other. I realize that, for a long time, albeit as subtly as I can, I have tried to force her to look up and to induce her to emerge from her defences – which she needs in order to avoid the catastrophic sensation that caused her to stop speaking to anyone except her mother. Alice concretely shows the world how alone she is, perhaps in the hope that someone will help her to confront the blockage in which the defences have taken the place of what never was – of what was unable to create the ability to relate. For Alice, not speaking signifies the concrete communication of being unable to fill the space of distance symbolically, of lacking the instruments to confront an object loss felt to be catastrophic. I feel that I am sharing with her the anxiety of being together in a room where she feels unable or unwilling to speak so as to oppose what everyone, including myself, wants from her. I now propose to try to make this space disappear by turning the setting that guarantees our meetings the other way round, although I do not really know how and to what extent this may affect the process of transformation of our unconscious emotions. Having obtained her parents' permission, in the next session, I suggest to Alice that we go out into the street to photograph her feet as she walks. In the street, I again find myself thinking about my possible responsibility in the event of an accident, and I myself feel vulnerable and insecure.

I am always extremely reluctant to vary the setting, for several good reasons. Disobeying the rules of the setting as developed in the theory of technique to guarantee analytic security for patient and therapist alike is therefore subject to powerful inhibitions and very painful, so at first I feel very inadequate and afraid of catastrophic accidents. For this reason, while we are walking, I also have a painful and sometimes terrifying sense of being subject to coercion; I imagine that these feelings are similar to Alice's when I try to tear her away from her setting – that is, the closed, silent room in which she lives. On returning to my office, we upload the photographs to the computer, yielding a photo reportage in which I see from her perspective holes, disconnected paving stones, drains, stunted blades of grass looking for cracks in which to grow and fragments of pedestrian crossings. I observe urban landscapes that sprout from beneath her tennis shoes, which tell me more than words about her state of mind: the wish to trample on everything and everyone and the fragility of having to maintain a balance with the maelstrom that is the world (see Figure 5.1). Alice feels that she is the protagonist in showing me something of herself by way of her skill in producing photographs of good technical quality – that is, in speaking in images. When the photographs have been printed, I watch as they are selected, as some of them are deleted and as she timidly seeks to put them in an aesthetically satisfying order. As she does all this, Alice whispers almost imperceptibly, 'Like this'. She means 'putting them

Figure 5.1 Under Alice's shoes

together like this', but I also imagine that she is referring to the experience of a creative side of herself and the establishment of some level of communication.

These actions seem to have led Alice into an area of the mind where lies the roots of relationship, where touch and sight fill the gap between self and other and where the perception of one's space while walking summons up the archaic experience in which space was first and foremost the experience of an anxiety-inducing distance separating the child from the mother's arms.[11] What first surprised me was that the holding function contained in the setting was paradoxically achieved in an open space and in a variation of the setting rhythm. This turning round of the concrete setting, which originated in the anteroom, and its comparison with a mental device with analogous effects to the camera obscura, made me wonder what had hitherto prevented the birth of a function whereby both my own and Alice's primitive anxieties could be symbolized. I wondered whether the classical setting always sufficed to apprehend both the primitive and the deeply buried. Alice's symptom is situated at a primitive level of development, and my adult mental functioning finds it very difficult to attune itself to these early developmental levels. I need a different mental approach from the one I normally use in the consulting room – a kind of anteroom enabling me to draw closer to a part of myself of which I am entirely unconscious. *"I think that when we use the word 'deep' we always imply deep in the patient's unconscious fantasy or psychic reality: that is to say, the patient's mind and imagination are involved"*.[12]

Primitive refers to an experience in which the conditions required for a mind to distinguish between conscious and unconscious have not yet arisen; their establishment depends on appropriate development of a child's early relationships. Sensory, emotionally primary consciousness, or, as Bion calls it, *"rudimentary"* consciousness, is not associated with an unconscious,[13] and for this reason, Alice needs a considerable number of therapeutic interventions directed towards constructing the mental container and developing the α function rather than probing its functioning. For what underlies extreme defences is the interruption of the psychic functions of thinking, which met early on with a blockage in the capacity to create relational links, thus compromising affective and cognitive development. In these cases, analytic therapy is called upon to recreate an environment and interactions permitting a rerun of the stages of primal psychic experience. With all due caution having regard to the examples – and failures – of the past, can we today think of possible variations of the setting to help us explore areas of the analytic field that cannot readily be reached in the classical setting, which has come to be structured as an approach for individuals who can speak? Can younger or older children who do not speak or play benefit more from settings other than those hitherto applied in the analyst's consulting room?

My variation of the setting has in a sense enabled the minds of analyst and patient to meet in an extraterritorial location of the field; that is to say, we were both in practice disobeying the obligation to observe the commonsense rules of our respective groups that made for security.[14] Leaving the consulting room enabled us potentially to experience the preconditions for what Bion calls the development of a physical and emotional *"common sense"*.[15] The first step in this direction was, perhaps not coincidentally, that of turning the other way round – when I focused on the patient's feet instead of her head. This shift involved a sensory sharing of experience and triggered an initial transformation of a mass of sense data that could not be represented in the consulting room. In proposing that we leave the room, I thought it might be possible to adopt Alice's visual perspective, but when I actually did so, the fear of setting off in a dangerous direction became equally concrete, thus favouring a physical and emotional consensual experience with my young patient. In addition, my experience in the anteroom when Alice began to talk to her mother must have triggered something personal in myself. My patient and I had turned things the other way round in the sense of unconsciously exchanging roles. An infantile part of myself must have enjoyed the idea of an exclusive relationship, which I had somehow offered to Alice in the form of something absolutely special. The variation of the setting was the "*maternal illness*" that enabled both of us to re-establish a function of development. Alice was able to lead me into a camera obscura, in which I was surprised by an image that took an unexpected shape, and afterwards, she was able to be surprised in my presence.

Giovanni: the focal distance and the flattened image

Mr D is the father of a child in analytic treatment. Mr D and I have an extremely bad relationship with each other. Despite all my efforts to believe that his attitude results from a defensive armour, this gentleman sorely tries my ability to tolerate him, especially when, at the end of a session, I am in the anteroom and still profoundly identified with his son and quite unwilling to listen to the other, equally traumatized, child concealed within the father. The following brief dialogue indicates what I tend to find intolerable:

Child: "Daddy, have a look at the house we have played!"
Father: "You can't say that because 'to play' is an intransitive verb. Repeat 'in-transitive' . . . and then watch out . . . And your cap is on the wrong way round again! How many times must I tell you how to put it on right, but you never learn anything! I keep telling you, but it's a waste of time, anyone would think you were mentally deficient."

Considering that Giovanni is five years old, it is easy to see that the use of incomprehensible words and the inability to attune emotionally to an as yet imperfect competence each time have the effect of an icy-cold shower on both the child and myself.

Without a conscious decision, it so happened that, as the weeks passed, at the end of his sessions, I began to help Giovanni put on his hat and coat before leaving the playroom so that I could return him to his father in the anteroom, ready to leave the building in a way that limited our interactions to the essential minimum. The anteroom thus became an intransitive place – that is, a place unsuitable for the negotiation of not readily tolerable conflict.

In a session just before Christmas, both parents come along with Giovanni and stay behind to wait for him. At the end of the session, when Giovanni and I leave the children's room, the mother appears in the anteroom and Giovanni embraces her. At this point, the father leaps out of the waiting room as if wanting to play hide-and-seek. Giovanni catches a fright, and, already slightly off balance from embracing his mother, falls to the floor, dragging his mother down with him. We then all find ourselves bending over the child in a strange, less hostile proximity. 'We all fell down', I say, thinking of ring-around-a-rosy. This is not intended as an analytic intervention, nor do I wish to describe either how the parents relate to the child or the possible meaning of what has just happened. My utterance has to do with me personally; it is perhaps the unconscious response to my surprise at the hint of a game introduced by the father, with the infantile scene of disarranged bodies accidentally in contact with one another that we have staged. Just for a moment, this odious gentleman and I have found ourselves in a play space where neither he nor I needed to demonstrate anything to the other. That evening, I recall a game that Giovanni has repeatedly wanted to play with me. When we paint with tempera, he likes first of all to stick some pieces of Scotch tape onto the paper. What happens when he then starts to paint is that the colour tends to seep through the slippery surface of the tape, causing smudges that blur the division of the space for painting. It then occurs to me that dressing Giovanni for the street was intended to avoid hassle – it was an attempt to distinguish sharply between the space of a behaviour deemed appropriate (mine) and one felt to be inappropriate (the father's). This presumption had accentuated the normal sense of rivalry felt in his heart by any parent compelled to use a therapist for his child and a sense of superiority which is always likely to insinuate itself into the therapist against his conscious will. The problem that seemed to me to be the other's became intolerable owing to my active participation in its creation.

The point I wish to make here is that in the anteroom – that is, where we had concretely come together as a group – the child had demonstrated to me his capacity to influence his parents by triggering an affectionate impulse in both. The reduction of the distance between us and the actual situation of being off balance with respect to my relational schemata enables me to visualize how the child had already apprehended an element of the group analytic field whereby the unconscious relationship that united us could be described. I then used the child's drawing to introduce, into the field of relationship with the parents, the effective representation by which the child had been able to act as the probe of the unconscious group field – an extremely sensitive probe for detection of a problem in which each of us ultimately colluded.[16]

A family: a landscape too wide-ranging to be confined within a room

'Pardon me, doctor, do you by any chance have a diaper?' These words are addressed to me at the door after an initial consultation. The problem brought to me by the lady and her husband concerns their eldest son, but since she is breastfeeding and they have come from relatively far away, they have come to the consultation together with their baby daughter, who is just a few months old. At first, it takes a few seconds for me to get my bearings; then the mother gestures toward the baby in the child's seat. I understand and politely reply that I do not have any diapers. When, next day, I decide to take some notes on the consultation, the surprise I had felt in the anteroom on the previous evening begins to take on a wider significance.

First, I am more aware of the form of their arrival: 'My husband dropped us off and went to park the car; he'll be here in a moment', the wife had begun, in explanation of her husband's momentary absence. Although it is in fact not difficult to park near my office at that time of the day, the husband had not joined us for a good half hour. In the meantime, the wife had described the behavioural and language difficulties of their elder child to me. According to her account, these difficulties were bound up with the twofold trauma that had afflicted him when he started school: separation from the grandmother who had cared for him until then and separation from his diapers. For since the child had, according to the mother, not yet mastered sphincter control, this drastic demand had in her view given rise to humiliation on several occasions. The father, who had meanwhile joined us, had told me that a previous therapy had been broken off because the boy did not like being observed. Since the family's provisional explanations of their child's difficulties in terms of direct causality had, even while I listened to them, seemed to me somewhat simplistic, the little appendix to the dialogue in the anteroom played a fundamental part in helping me to put certain things together and assign at least a provisional meaning to them.

It seemed to me that the protagonists had in various ways invited me to understand that there was both an overflowing and a void that they found difficult to handle. I had experienced this in the first part of the consultation, when the constant interruption due to the mother's caring for the crying infant and the account of the elder child's difficulties had made me feel that so many demands were being made on me that I was quite unable to think. Thereafter, every so often, I found myself looking at the empty chair waiting for the father and wondering where he might have ended up. The theory they had thought up to explain their child's problem once again suggested an unexpected deficiency of caring and the absence of a diaper to absorb evacuations.

At the door, they had given me the key to embarking on the therapy without being immediately evacuated, since the father had dropped off[17] mother and daughter and then explained to me that he absolutely did not want to be observed. I was therefore required to become a diaper, to receive and absorb the toxic fluids disseminated in the form of various kinds of action, which eventually, in the older child, became a disorder of language and behaviour.

As to the setting, it seems to me that, had I suggested a form of observation or therapy to the father, the consultation would not have been followed up, whereas receiving the mother and daughter would represent collusion with the failure to listen to an infantile part of the father. A decision to see the child a few times together with the mother or by himself on the basis of a shared consultation might have been understood as a refuge that immediately laid down unacceptable rules. My eventual choice of a relatively passive setting was guided by these considerations. I told them that we could decide on each occasion when to meet and that they could take turns to come, or they could come together, with or without the children as they saw fit.

The anteroom as a creative place

Imagining the anteroom (anticamera) as a place similar to a camera obscura, I have presented some examples of how the psychic reality that manifests itself in this space can facilitate the observation of phenomena that are not visible in the kind of analytic field arising in the consulting room. After all, when patient and analyst are together in the consulting room, they generate a highly intense conscious and unconscious emotional field of forces. The analyst is in a state of receptive availability and on the lookout for any verbal or non-verbal signal; analyst and patient alike are involved in an exploratory situation in which each exerts a powerful influence on the other. Although we are not emotionally unavailable in the anteroom, our level of emotional availability is certainly different. Being alone in the presence of someone makes it possible for both patient and analyst to gain access to emotional experiences which may be less readily contactable, for reasons for collusion, in the field established in the consulting room.

These clinical examples, in my view, illustrate several phenomena.

a. The setting is in effect a device that regulates the focal distance between the two subjects in the analytic relationship. The internal and external setting, as it has come to be structured and as we have learned to use it, has many advantages, but the rigidity of this frame may make it impossible to get in touch with certain phenomena. We are now in a position to try out settings different from those of psychoanalysis in its more classical form. The range of possible settings includes what happens in the anteroom, the text messages often sent to us by patients, sessions via Skype or, as described earlier, brief forays outside the consulting room. Among the first painters to use the device of the camera obscura to bring out certain aspects of their talent was Vermeer. He used it to emphasize the effects of light in the various focal planes of the scene portrayed. I believe that, like Vermeer, Alice showed me her talent in demonstrating her unconscious gift for representation and was able to do so when we agreed to apply an artifice of the setting to explore what had become visible in the anteroom as a fluid, wrong-way-round image. By surprising each other, each of us was then able to take a step in the direction of exploring the unknown.

b. In the case of Giovanni, the anteroom was the place in which I was able to experience an out-of-place sensation analogous to that noticed when observing works by painters who have used optical aids. In some of these paintings, the device had to be moved, so that, on closer inspection, the image of the model appears slightly unnatural or with inconsistent details. These are, of course, only details, and the out-of-place sensation mostly remains subliminal but becomes obvious when the correct image is observed. In Giovanni's case, the unnatural sensation had become more evident in the anteroom, and I had originally felt that it might have to do with this father's difficulty of relating to his child. What was unnatural, however, was my involuntary but annoying substitution of myself for the parental function, which had resulted in our relationship being painted in vivid colours stemming from profound anxieties and an intense unconscious conflict. Yet it was only in a virtually extra analytic situation that we were able to observe the situation we were constructing and to realize how the anteroom had played a decisive part in our ability to observe. In the anteroom, I had become more aware of my hatred for the father and my resulting out-of-place position in relation to the parents. This perception had been favoured by the child's ability to represent unconscious aspects of the group and of my relationship with the parents, but it was only in the anteroom that these compositional elements had emerged into the light of day and become accessible to perception and consciousness.

c. In the last example, the anteroom becomes the space in which a wider view can be discerned of the psychic dynamic of the entire family group – a dynamic in which the therapist was co-opted with effect from the very first meeting. In this case, too, it is the patient who, albeit unawares, supplies the focal point upon which a complex landscape converges. Here, the anteroom is analogous to the process applied by Canaletto in reducing an overextensive view to the dimensions of a canvas by optical means. This involves a kind of compression or reduction of longitudinal spaces in such a way that the canvas can accommodate a wider view than would be possible for the naked eye.

The camera obscura was at first regarded as an instrument that could supersede the skill of the painter and allow anyone to reproduce reality. Similarly, I believe that carefully chosen alternative settings can permit the exploration of areas that cannot be reached in the strictly classical situation. When patients request a variation of the setting, we must in my view beware of collusion and avoid acting out, which would prevent us from grasping what is actually happening. However, if our posture is not one of suspicion and we regard the patient as our best colleague, discreet variations of the classical setting may well constitute a new adaptation of this device, which has hitherto helped us to apprehend psychic phenomena, but which can, precisely for this reason, be complemented by further instruments permitting new representations. The setting, after all, can be seen as a probe for exploration of the field – a probe that is in turn modified by the field it is exploring.

Notes

1 *Anticamera* in Italian; hence the comparison with a camera obscura.
2 For convenience, the masculine form is used for both sexes throughout the case of this chapter.
3 Winnicott 1964b, p. 33.
4 Hockney 2001.
5 Winnicott 1958c; Modell 1976, 1989; Civitarese 2010.
6 Bleger 1967, Ogden 1992, Greenberg 2012.
7 Ferro and Basile 2006, Grotstein 2009, Brown 2015.
8 Meltzer 1967, Ogden 2004b, p. 1357.
9 Ambrosiano 1998, Nissim Momigliano 1988.
10 Schacht 2000, Winnicott 1971.
11 Milner 1950, p. 13.
12 Winnicott 1964a, p. 111.
13 Bion 1967, p. 117.
14 Bion used the common sense with different meanings. I use two of them. The first: the capacity to maintain an agreement with the tenet of the group is necessary to survive. If an individual cannot maintain a common sense with the group, then he has to face his fear of the group (Bion 1992, p. 29).
15 The second: common sense in the sense of a "*common emotional vision, a sense of truth is experienced if the view of an object which is hated can be conjoined to a view of the same object when it is loved*" (Bion 1967, p. 119).
16 Molinari 2013b.
17 The Italian word *scaricato* also means 'discharged' in the sense of evacuation or excretion.

Chapter 6

The use of child drawings to explore the dual ↔ group analytic field in child analysis

During the first meetings of a child therapy, the analyst finds himself – even before seeing the child – confronted with the parents and with the story of how they have tried to understand and transform the ailment that has motivated them to ask for help. Awareness that the child is part of a complex relational and fantasied system has ensured that all child analysts, though belonging to different lines of thought, agree on the necessity of establishing a therapeutic alliance with the parents, and towards this end, they have developed different techniques of involving the family.[1]

The family entrusts the child, through symptomatology, with the role of mouthpiece for voicing complex conflictual dynamics. Extended analytic work has proven useful in pointing out the transgenerational unconscious mandate[2] with which to re-establish or create for the first time moments of enzymatic emotional attunement of a larger-scale relational transformation[3] or to encourage the construction of an imaginary place where this attunement can be born for the first time.[4]

What I intend to highlight is that unconscious conflictual dynamics may involve the analyst starting from the moment of consultation and may immediately draw him into an analytic field that is much closer to that of a group than to the bi-personal set-up of therapy with adults. In particular, utilizing a clinical example, it is possible to grasp how, through play and drawings, the child may be capable of exploring and mapping not only the unconscious relationship established between himself and the analyst but also the extended analytic field that is generated. This includes the unconscious relationship between the analyst and the parents as well. In my opinion, the child ends up being the most susceptible member of the group but also the one who can catalyse the transformation into dreaming of unprocessed emotions and of feelings that interfere with his smooth functioning.

During analysis, the child develops the capacity to symbolize some of these group dynamics, especially when his games and drawings have as their content the family or groups of persons in relation to one another. The child's symbolic productions are strongly anchored in sensory and aesthetic elements and can be used as a powerful activator of a transformative process in the group.

The symptom's 'ice age'

Elisa, a five-year-old child, is brought to a consultation because she does not chew her food. In the first meeting, her parents tell me that Elisa will not eat any solid food, and at preschool, where she is not given any alternatives, she regularly fasts. They tell me that her favourite food is Nutella.[5] They would like me to give them some advice, or, even better, to give them a quick method of convincing Elisa to taste something solid. Unfortunately, I have no shortcuts, and I confine myself to listening attentively to all the desperate attempts devised by the parents as well as those suggested by others, all of which have failed miserably. At the end of this first meeting, with the aim of saying something judicious, I propose some observational sessions with Elisa and an additional session with them. A few days later, Elisa arrives with her father, and together, we go into the playroom.

Elisa: "Let's take the mammoth [Manfred], and we'll play Ice Age. You can take Sid [the sloth] – no, wait, you take Diego [the sabre-toothed tiger]!" In a thoughtful tone, she adds, "Um, you can take both of them."
Then she takes a large boy doll and decisively announces, "I'll take the boy!"
In a thin voice, almost as though to convey a great secret, she whispers, "If you are Diego, you really don't want to take the boy back to the humans, you want to kill him!"
Analyst: "I want to kill him?"
Elisa: "Yes, of course – because you are very angry with his father and now you want to kill everyone!"

Elisa's father intervenes, rebuking Elisa by telling her she must not say such things. "Look here," he says to me. "She is rather an insolent child, and she often wants to play boys' games."

Elisa proposes that we play a game inspired by the 2002 movie *Ice Age*. In the film, a strange trio of animals – a mammoth, a sloth and a sabre-toothed tiger – find themselves together by chance. They are on a journey that takes them in search of food and rescue from an impending ice age. During the journey, Manfred, the mammoth, rescues a little boy, the adored son of a mother who tried to save him from the risk of being kidnapped but died in the attempt. Behind the kidnapping plot lurks Diego, the sabre-toothed tiger, who acts on behalf of his own group, which has been decimated by hunters – among whom was the boy's father. Motivated by revenge, Diego must kill the boy, and this is why he pretends to ally himself with his other two travelling companions, who intend to return the child to the humans.

Reflecting on the game, I think that Elisa may be having some difficulty in managing her aggression, as perhaps her father is as well. I hypothesize that the father perceives Elisa's game as unacceptable, too explicit in terms of the hatred that he, too, can feel towards me. At that moment, I do not know how to communicate this hypothesis in a therapeutic way, and I decide not to say anything about my thoughts.

After the third meeting, the parents cancel an appointment and agree on another one but then do not arrive. Some days later, I contact them by phone, and the mother tells me that, under pressure from her husband, they have decided 'to change methods'. I am left feeling bewildered and am forced to review critically what might have happened. Every child analyst knows from experience about the ambivalence that parents harbour towards therapy, and if, on the one hand, they are desirous of a transformation, on the other, they often ask the therapist to cure without curing. The frequency of the sessions and the fees, the beginning as well as the end of the analysis, are all aspects that are clearly criss-crossed with these sentiments.[6] I rely on this prefabricated attribution of responsibility for the interruption to the parents in order to elude the aversion that the father has aroused in me.[7] To be able to use the ambivalence and hatred that I, too, feel towards him in particular would involve a painful examination of my unconscious countertransference, an undertaking that carries a high emotional cost and is for now impossible.

In the following weeks, the thought of this interruption forces me to reflect on the role of hate in the countertransference.[8] In a variation on a theme of Winnicott's, I arrive at the thought that sometimes the analyst can hate the parents before the parents hate the analyst and before the parents can know that the analyst hates them.[9]

This overturning of perspective allows me to incorporate myself more deeply in the process. I imagine Elisa's therapy as the journey of a group of people who are initially trying to escape together from the danger of a glacialized symptom entrusted to the child and then attempt to survive an equally perilous thawing of those unconscious emotions that have generated it.

The analyst-sloth

The first character that Elisa had assigned to me in the game was that of Syd, the sloth. On re-watching the film, I found an exchange of retorts between Manfred and Syd ironically pertinent:

Manfred: "You're an expert at following tracks, right?"
Syd: "Hey, I'm a sloth – I see a tree, I eat the leaves, and that's the end of the tracks!"

At my first meeting with Elisa's parents, they had explicitly asked me to be quick, to tell them something new that would at least alleviate some of their anxiety about having a daughter who was different from all the other children. Among their fantasies was that Elisa might have some mysterious illness – even though all the examinations and tests carried out at the suggestion of their paediatrician had excluded physiological problems. Faced with such urgent distress, my non-response and the proposal of further innumerable sessions could not but disappoint them. I realized that I had followed the theoretical canon on how to do a parent-child consultation, and I had anchored myself in the very psychoanalytic idea that slowness and reflection are essential elements of good practice. I had barricaded myself within a theory that had made me nearsighted, causing certain aspects of our meetings – starting with the spatio-temporal ones of the setting – to appear obvious and natural. In this way, I had lost sight of the emotional tracks that these parents left behind in their discourse aimed at explaining the problem to me.[10] It is also possible that my slowness may have been an early unconscious reaction to a feeling of pressure that these parents caused me to experience through the agitated rhythm and the continual, irritating superimposition of their discourse. At a certain point, I had detached the audio portion of their communication, and for some seconds, I found myself observing them as though I were wearing earplugs. Inside my head, I was hearing the song "Too Much Love Will Kill You" by Freddy Mercury. I chased away these fantasies as an annoying distraction and resumed listening.

It is necessary to have a great deal of trust in the capacity of one's own α function to create pictograms of unconscious emotions – trust and the readiness to utilize these images in order to *"talk-as-dreaming"*.[11] Thus, it is understandable that these details emerged into my consciousness only after the interruption.

The analyst-mammoth: the heaviness

Instances of parental lack necessarily reverberate in the analyst's internal world and reactivate the pain and hatred of the analyst's own wounds. The resultant identification with the child implies that the missing elements of his environment, or the attitudes of sometimes explicit mistreatment, come to be felt as hateful. The risk for the child analyst, then, is that he may find himself in an emotionally very turbulent place, in which defences are easily activated that can make themselves evident in critical thoughts towards the parents' educational difficulties or in an indignant distancing from the lack of psychic containment. If he does not set up an attentive vigilance against this type of experience, the analyst risks feeling that he is the child's saviour, and at the same time, that he is burdened by the weight of internally reciting this dialogue:

Syd: "We'll take him [the child] back to them!"
Manfred: "Let's be sure we understand each other. Don't talk in the plural – there's no we. In fact, without me, there wouldn't even be a you!"

I think that we should regain an analytic lightness, applying to the parents' story what Ferro[12] suggests doing with respect to the patient's real story. If we try mentally placing the phrase *"You know, I had a dream in which . . ."* before whatever the patient relates, then we are more apt to succeed in listening analytically to the anamnestic story that the parents tell us. If we consider them as members of a group, and thus place ourselves in the position of having a group viewpoint, then we can think that every story, even the most real one, may also be mapping conscious and unconscious emotions present in the field – including the unconscious emotion aroused by the meeting with the analyst. From this perspective, the story of a little girl who fasts would have permitted me to listen to the hunger of a small part of the parents as well. They were ravenous, angry and anxious to receive advice or – even more so – to receive a nurturing response with respect to their capacity to be parents.

The analyst-sabre-toothed tiger

Too much love will kill you – my mind had provided an extremely valuable clue with which to orient myself both internally and externally. If I could have listened to my annoyance in response to the parents' agitated discussions, perhaps I would have intuited that, in my heart, I had already identified with this little girl whose oppositional capacities caused me to feel a great deal of sympathy. I thought with satisfaction that she had been able to resist blackmail of the worst kind, and a secret part of me admired her and was her fan. Elisa was capable of taking in and defending my childhood protest, and this identification had even modified the perception of the sound of words. From that perspective, the parents' words reached me as though I had earphones on – that is, as little more than background noise, as a child often perceives adult discourse. From this vantage point of identification with the child, in an as yet unaware way, I must have started to feel a certain hatred towards those parents. Not acting on one's feelings is a product of analytic training, but learning to use those feelings, and especially to transform them into words that do not inflict harm, is always a creative task that one undertakes as a novice.

I had conceived the idea that the mother was more capable of observing Elisa, of making connections with the emotions that the child could feel, while the father had pestered me – both in our conversations and in the play sessions with Elisa – with questions about how they could deceive Elisa:

> What do you think about our buying a blender that chops up food but doesn't exactly blend it? What do you think of the Bimbi brand? And

what if we use pieces of bread that we've soaked in liquid, but that don't completely dissolve?

I was unsuccessful in holding him back. I did not succeed in thinking either and, in the sessions as in our conversations, I simply tried to reach the end of the hour with dignity and to secure another appointment, hoping to be in better condition the next time. In the sessions, I could have again said something 'well blended', as he had suggested to me, or I could have slipped into the word *blender* a little piece – partially hidden – of interpretation of my hatred and his own. At the shared observational sessions, Elisa's mother was never present due to unpredictable problems at her job. From a group point of view – which, after the interruption, I felt I grasped more clearly – I asked myself whether this exclusion could also be a signal of the absence of my own maternal aspects capable of a real acceptance of difficult emotions, without the excuse of an analytic job.

Learning to be a herd

Diego: "Why did you do it?"
Manny: "Because one does such things in a herd."

This brief dialogue contains traces of an early transformation of the hatred that, in the movie, supports the tiger's mandate to kill the child. Ethologically, the herd defines itself as a sort of big family composed of both sexes. The herd moves, hunts and feeds itself together, and all the members cooperate in the defence and care of the offspring.

With a little imagination, child therapy can be considered to have the aim of supporting a youngster in difficulty, and it is composed of a herd of adults who try to learn to cooperate among themselves. I deliberately use the word *herd* because, in therapy, in addition to the real persons who form a small group, others are present in fantasy: siblings and members of preceding generations (and perhaps also of future ones). The interruption of treatment and the sole, enigmatic explanation that was given to me – that is, the father's need to 'change methods' – continually came back to my mind, pressuring me to create an explanatory hypothesis.

After some months, the mother called me again, explaining that they had decided to return because Elisa had asked to have for her birthday the same little wooden house that I have in my office. This possibility of once again sharing a common house or home was a gift for me, too. The parents initially accepted twice-weekly therapy for Elisa as well as a monthly meeting between the two of them and me. Thus, it was they themselves who found the 'method' of continuing, bringing to the first meeting a drawing of Elisa's in order to show me how she tyrannized them (see Figure 6.1).

They explained to me that, in the drawing, Elisa had drawn herself on her father's side of the big bed and that it often happened like that: until they agreed to her taking over their bed, Elisa would not go to sleep. Her father told me that the light fixture in the drawing reminded him of a circus routine they had seen in which a knife-thrower hurled knives at a live person, and, in a certain sense, Elisa was aiming knives at him, really killing him, with that fixation about not chewing. I looked at the drawing and thought that a childhood aspect of all of us had occupied the field in an overbearing way.

Figure 6.1 Room of Elisa's parents

In the mother with her back turned, I saw my own sadness and scornful rage, aroused in me by the feeling of being rejected. The exclusion of maternal aspects, as I mentioned, had already entered into the field with the problematic absence of the mother during our joint observation sessions. But now, through the drawing, the problem of exclusion became something that pertained to each of us.

In the drawing, Elisa had made this greater emotional awareness possible through the formal aspect of her composition. I thought that at the bottom of the hatred – which exclusion involves – there is always a sense of being pushed to the margins. Elisa carefully avoided the movement of pushing food to one side of her mouth between her teeth, almost as though searching for a motoric expression of an emotionally painful sensation. We talked about the drawing in simple terms, utilizing her expressive capacity to share – each in our own way – fragments of awareness that the most primitive bonds are bodily ones and that their loosening may produce a measure of very intense hatred.[13]

The association the father had made to the knife-thrower seemed to me to carry something disquieting, something more radical than the normal emotional vicissitudes that accompany the relative exclusion of the child from the parental couple. Something of those knives had been manifest in the clean break with which the therapy had been interrupted before it was even born. I told them that perhaps Elisa had felt in their room as though she were in the Garden of Eden – until the day when she had doubted their unconditional welcome or they had felt able to cut back on being tyrannized. In retrospect, I can imagine that my reference to Eden was a way of alluding to something at a very early point of development. While the difficulty we adults had in relating had been apparent in the interruption of treatment – beneath which there seemed to be a feeling of hatred that was in part reciprocated – Elisa's symptom expressed a more primitive emotion than hatred. The freeze on chewing could have been a symptom of a love that was so voracious that, in fantasy, the child feared she could destroy the object, as happens in schizoid disturbances.[14] The projection of this type of love generates, then, a ravenous mode that risks devouring the sense of self and simultaneously negating oral needs.[15]

What began to appear evident to me, considering the group point of view, was that we were in a situation in which psychological investigation had caused the emergence of a *"protomental system"* that was located in an undifferentiated state between the physical and the mental, and from this matrix, the basic assumptions that had dominated the beginning of the therapy had been born.[16]

I told the parents that Elisa's drawing probably contained a seed of development (implicit in the figures) and at the same time the traces of an anxiety that had made all of them feel bad. At that moment, I did not know how to say much more to them. At the end of the meeting, however, I had the distinct feeling that a communicative situation had been created, and I told them that this 'method' of thinking together seemed intense to me, and that, if Elisa did other drawings of the family, I, too, would share them. At the next meeting, which took place about a month later, I showed them a drawing that Elisa had done in a session (see Figure 6.2).

Figure 6.2 Parents at work

Elisa explained to me that, in this drawing, she had portrayed her parents at work: her father was bent over his desk; her mother was doing housework, and, at the bottom of the drawing, was shown running to buy Nutella. In the session, I thought that Elisa was representing various levels of her feelings: the pleasure of tyrannizing her mother through food, the dawning perception of her capacity to move psychically in two different modes (a more reflective one and a more action-oriented one), the hardship of experiencing the disappearance of the other or simply the separation conveyed in the drawing by the difficulty of portraying the mother while she was going out. In addition, the drawing could also represent the two modalities in which Elisa could perceive our being there and not being there inside the analytic process.

In the session, I had used precisely this unusual uncertainty of hers expressed in the drawing to tell her that, when she felt left alone – as, for example, when her parents left her at preschool to go to work – she might be angry, and the anger was something that upset all the usual rules or in certain moments could cause the emergence of a wish to erase everything. Elisa had listened to this interpretation, pointing out that, in the drawing, her mother was leaving to go and buy Nutella. In working with Elisa, I followed the classical dual-relation technique, and so I returned with her many times during the therapy to interpreting to her, through play, the drawing and the interaction between emerging aspects of her psychic difficulties.

What I intend to point out in this chapter is how group work contributed to the recognition of psychic difficulties by each of its members. I did not intend to use the drawing shown in Figure 6.2 with the parents to demonstrate what happened in analysis, even though the sharing of something that happens in the intimacy of the analytic relationship between analyst and child may alleviate a parental sense of exclusion. The way in which I intended to use Elisa's drawings was to be able to look at them in continuing the process of getting to know one another that had started up among us, as a group.

The title 'Parents at Work' that Elisa had given to her drawing seemed significant to me for its possible use in this new method that we were exploring. I told the parents simply that Elisa saw them like this while they were working. The parents began to talk about their work and seemed comforted by how I took into account their considerable efforts and obligations as people and as parents. The mother thought that Elisa had drawn her as she was stumbling because this was something that happened to her often. Almost a little tangentially, she said that Elisa's symptom had made her 'stumble like Mommy'. At this point, she began to speak as though quite distressed. She related that, once when she was little, she had happened to stumble and accidentally killed a baby chick. She described how she had crushed its little neck and had felt an indescribable horror. She had run away, crying, and had hidden for hours; she had not dared to confess her crime to anyone. From then on, she remained obsessed with the idea of stumbling, and when Elisa was little and she carried her in her arms, she had always been very afraid of falling and crushing her.

I thought that this woman was beginning to be able to say something about the difficulty and the hatred that a child arouses in every mother. To me, her narration about it seemed particularly strengthening of the links that she had managed to express among some perceptive aspects, bodily sensations and emotions. Her memory had produced a revealing narration of an experience that can provoke hatred: a sense of loss of equilibrium and a catastrophic perception of its consequences. It is possible that these parents were trying to make me understand emotionally how they had felt crushed at the beginning (as children in our story) by me and how my exclusion had been the only strategy for a temporary rescue. To mitigate the dense climate of pain that had been created, the father recounted that, as a children's game, he had once organized the funeral of some dead animals. He talked of how his companions at primary school had staged the burial during recess of a wasp that the children themselves had killed during the lesson.

I had the feeling that the parents were deeply intuiting something of the emotion that underlay Elisa's symptom, and I participated emotionally in their stories but without setting myself the objective of interpreting before a shared meaning could emerge. When we work on schizoid aspects instead of neurotic personality ones, it is appropriate to wait for the patient to find meaning; the interpretive fruit of the analyst's ability and experience in these cases comes to be systematically refused and destroyed.[17] I think that in this phase, as Neri suggests, the analyst's task must be that of creating an emotional attunement and of *"encouraging the fact that the members of the group are uniting with the developing core"*.[18]

At the next meeting, the parents told me that they had celebrated their wedding anniversary, and Elisa had wanted to see their photograph album of the ceremony. Then she did a drawing (see Figure 6.3). Figuring out

Figure 6.3 Wedding of parents

two enlargements of the drawing (crocifisso e animali sovrapposti) demonstrate how the representation of anger and death became possible for Elisa in relation to the same capacity that was developing in her parents. This representation was combined with the possibility of representing the loving bond as well. The parents commented especially on Elisa's passion for animals and on how there was always something off the mark in her games and drawings, as in this drawing. We attentively observed the various animals, and with each of them, the parents did a sort of free-association exercise. In reality, I thought that the animals were not at all inappropriate; I thought again of the initial game of *Ice Age* – a game that Elisa had often taken up again, inspired both by subsequent episodes and by the introduction of many of her own fantastic variations. The idea of a herd of animals had at first helped me focus on the group-like nature of our relationship, and it continued to be a very useful element in observing how the oneiric work might bring together a multiplicity of emotions, both on an intrapsychic level and on an intersubjective one. Concentrating on this representation of a group of animals, among which there was a snake, I was moved to speak to them about how something instinctive had led them to seek help for Elisa's symptom. I related to them how I had happened to read that, during World War I, aboard the early rudimentary submarines, a sailor could succeed in locating an approaching ship by holding a monkey wrench in his mouth, with one end between his lips and the other supported by the wall of the submarine. Those sailors knew how to listen with their senses, and we would have to try to do this, too, from inside our own personal conflicts, in order to begin to understand not only something of Elisa's symptom but also what had reciprocally disappointed us at the beginning of the therapy. The parents and I continued to share our observations about the drawings on a monthly basis, or sometimes the story of a game that Elisa had created with me, with the same method described. The drawings or the story of the game allowed us to undergo a less defensive exploration and to achieve a greater attunement with the emotions and sensations present in each member of the group.

Much later in the therapy (which, after a year, became an analysis of three sessions per week), I learned some details of the parents' personal history that made me consider the little girl's early drawings and her symptom in a new way: as an extraordinary condensation of an unconscious mandate.

As Kaës writes, the unconscious is not entirely contained within the borders of the individual psychic space. The psychic space of the connection is another area of the unconscious, a type of unconscious that only the group could cause to emerge.[19]

The mother told me that she had become aware she was expecting in the sixth month of her pregnancy, and that, on learning from her doctor the source of the strange internal movements she had perceived, she had locked herself in her bedroom and tried to get rid of the child by violently hitting her abdomen with her fists. The feature of the murder of the boy in the initial game, and the crucifixion that dominated the parents' wedding in the drawing, can be considered clues to a denied lethal aspect, initially incorporated by Elisa in her refusal to feed herself – that is, chewing as a symbolic tearing into pieces. The mother's difficulty in accepting her pregnancy stemmed from, in turn, a very problematic relationship with her own mother and an equally difficult relationship with her husband, who had separated from a previous partner precisely on the occasion of Elisa's conception. He had reacted to her birth with a period of serious alcohol dependence. These grave relational difficulties emerged gradually, always through the free associations triggered by Elisa's drawings. Overall, it was the formal elements of the drawings (at times the composition and at other times the colours or some detail) that encouraged the emergence of conscious and unconscious personal contents. Those contents emerged at first in an indirect form, starting from a sensation, as happened with the story of the murdered chick that the mother had remembered through a sudden awareness of her fear of stumbling. This memory, which was also a waking dream capable of monitoring the unconscious emotions present in the intersubjective field, had emerged from the mother's personal interpretation of an oblique sign with which Elisa, in representing it, intended to give shape to running away. This sharing promoted – in the etymological sense of moving together towards something undefined – the emergence of unthought and unthinkable aspects as well as the unconscious alliances present among the group members.

As defined by Kaës, unconscious alliances permit the members of a group to reinforce in each some of the processes or functions or pathological structures from which each member profits for his own psychic stability. The family group, linked in this way through a negative pact, was able to maintain its psychic reality through the condition of reciprocal subjection of the members that make it up. In the initial interruption, one could hypothesize that the need for recruitment of another group member was being expressed – however, immediately declared dangerous to the psychic equilibrium of the group itself. To get out of an unconscious situation of this type, we had to face the possibility of making use of Elisa's drawings, applying the method of Bion's *"binocular vision"*[20] to them, which allowed us to see how (using Corrao's words) *"the mental phenomena constantly present a double side or a double face, each of which is manifested in two opposite fields and is at the same time connected, of the individual relations and of the group relations"*.[21] It seemed to me that the form of the drawing played an important role for two kinds of reasons: the first was that it condensed, as in a dream, elements of this group unconscious, including the conscious and unconscious experiences of the analyst. The second related to the iconic form that retained within the child's drawing an intense contact with bodily experiences, including incorporated unconscious ones.

This latter aspect held a key role in the possibility of knowing the protomental phenomena – that is, those phenomena that, born out of a system in which the physical and the mental exist in an undifferentiated state, appear in the group as distinct feelings, only slightly correlated among themselves. Bion[22] hypothesizes that it may be precisely from this matrix that the emotional states themselves originate from a basic assumption; these states reinforce, pervade and in some instances dominate the mental life of the group.

I will now present a final drawing from a more advanced phase of the therapy in order to demonstrate how this composite work on two levels,

Figure 6.4 Trip to the analyst's room

dual and group, could construct a space capable of hosting less conflictual relationships.

During a session, Elisa drew the trip she had made with her parents to come to my office. She portrayed the car in an intermediary way between reality and fantasy: initially, she told me that her father drove and that she and her mother were in the back seat. Then she added a coachman, transforming the car into a carriage (see Figure 6.4). She then dedicated herself to drawing various animals. The circus-like quality of some of the animals portrayed a sense of difficulty but also of an overturning of perspective that Elisa was confronting. The cat with his paws in the air in a position of trust, and the bond between the little birds that form a chain over the carriage, like the representation of various animals in couples, could be graphic expressions of a new psychic capacity for linking (L). The tying up of the horse represented, perhaps, this new capacity, together with the difficulty of containing ambivalent aspects.

When I again looked at this drawing together with the parents, they commented that Elisa had drawn the entire family. The father related this drawing to an early one of the parents' matrimonial bedroom because, he said, the drawing made him think of the film *Robin Hood*, seen a few days earlier with Elisa, in which a 'Just Married' sign appears at the end. He said that, with respect to the timing of the first drawing, now Elisa felt better with them. It seemed to me that the expression 'Just Married' could be the way in which the father expressed this new emotional attunement, together with a nascent capacity to be together.

In the drawing, the journey of coming to see me was represented, and the re-evocation of that first meeting brought to my mind the stormy beginning of this therapy. The monkey that bears a heavy balance wheel on his head made me live again the effort I had made to ensure that my curiosity prevailed over the crushing weight of a hatred that had been present in the consultation but with which I had strenuously struggled, later on as well. The somewhat acrobatic nature with which some of the animals were represented made me remember how the father had associated the light fixture of Elisa's first drawing to a routine performed at the circus by a knife-thrower. Now the free associations that emerged were not only less charged with anxiety but also more in tune with Elisa's portrayal. In the cats with lowered heads, the parents saw Elisa's stubbornness; in many life situations, she wanted to do exactly the opposite of what they proposed. In the meantime, however, the hatred had moved from the body to the relationship, and Elisa ate her food in small pieces.

Scrat and the elusive acorn

Scrat is a minor character in the film *Ice Age*; he is a comical squirrel-mouse who is obsessed by the wish to gather and store acorns that continually slip out of his hands, causing him to embark on daring adventures. This character, too, at a certain point had entered into the game Elisa proposed to me, taking her inspiration from the movie.

Two aspects of Scrat's presence struck me: it made me aware of how I, too, had had the experience many times – especially at the beginning of the therapy – of having something in my hands that was emotionally precious and useful, and, an instant later, this feeling had gone back to being shapeless, unthinkable. The other aspect is that I remembered that Nutella was Elisa's one redeeming food in her moments of stubborn fasting.

Nutella is a word composed of *nut* and the suffix *ella*, which in Italian is used in many words that have to do with the family and with food. Each in her own way, both Elisa and I longed to grasp the emotional nut that impeded our being a group. The character of Scrat accurately portrays how difficult it is to grasp a profound element of emotional truth rooted in an experience that never assumes a definite form.[23] The most fleeting part of the relational difficulty that we had both felt towards the other had to do with the emotional level close to withdrawal and death. This level was in some way expressed in the bodily language of Elisa's symptom. Normally when one eats, the food is constrained by the lips, torn to pieces by the teeth and rotated by the tongue, and only after a certain period of contact is it pushed down into the stomach. By contrast, Elisa made her food disappear inside herself without perceptive contact and almost without any movement if not that of swallowing. In this way, Elisa expressed not only her oppositional side but also the deepest part of hatred having to do with a radical passivity that implies the annihilation of perception that comes close to psychic death.[24]

In the group, on the other hand, these primitive aspects of non-contact were demonstrated through the interruption of the consultation – that is, with the sudden disappearance of the potentially nutritious element inherent in being able to think together. What I intend to emphasize is how the possibility of knowing at least in part this level of emotional truth may be placed at a juncture of an individual investigation by each of the subjects of the analysis but also of an emotional task of the group. In fact, work with the parents is not positioned – as sometimes happens – as a complementary aspect of therapy with the child but as an equal and parallel task. The dual-group oscillation[25] permitted the transfer of specific processing aspects from one to the other modality of analysis, with the effect of stabilization and of acceleration of the therapeutic process.

Reducing the difference between the child's therapy and the relationship with the parents

In the model of the field,[26] analytic work has the goal of broadening the field itself through an increase in the capacity for oneiric work of each of the subjects of analysis. The gradual involvement of the parents in child therapy is an ever more common practice, and hence the hypothesis that the analytic field is not a bi-personal one (analyst-child) but includes all the members of the familial group. What remains unexplored, however, is the method with which to continue – after the consultation – to share with the parents the level of creative attention that is experienced in playing when, by choice or by necessity, the play sessions are no longer shared.

The discovery that Elisa's game contained traces of one of my countertransferential sentiments towards her father led me to hypothesize that the drawings, like the game, could also be considered a tool with which to map the emotions present in an analytic field that extended beyond the analyst child couple. The drawings, then, were utilized as a probe with which to explore the universe of emotions that gathered in the field rather than being used in an explanatory sense. Elisa's drawings proved to be an efficient, attractive pathway in promoting the α function of each of the group members, and in this sense, they were an occasion through which the parents became more aware of their own unconscious emotions, which had been entrusted to Elisa and expressed through her symptomatology. The associations, memories and fantasies that grew up around the drawings permitted us to develop a new, unexpected capacity to play with images in the little group, without the necessity that they be directly interpreted as individual subjects.[27]

Exactly as happens in child analysis, in which play is a reparative process, generative of a psychic transformation of the self,[28] this method of utilizing drawings with the parents permitted the actualization with them of a relationship endowed with specific and non-specific therapeutic factors. In particular, the drawings, especially at the beginning, allowed the parents to feel affectively tuned in to their daughter, maintaining in the background the more ambivalent aspects of the relationship with me and avoiding their being acted out too directly. The work in a small group, in which Elisa was present through her productions, gradually permitted the putting together of these proto-representations, intentionally not interpreted in relation to Elisa and left in an unsaturated form until they could assume a shared meaning. The construction of a personal meaning for each member took place through the joining of his own associative chains with those of the other participants.[29]

From a more theoretical point of view, each member of the group could experience both a form of affective security through the investigation of his own subjective understanding of the drawing (transformation in K) and the exploration of a more disquieting emotional truth through an experience of shared creativity (transformation in O). The efficacy of this method, in my opinion, lies in the possibility of not expropriating the parents' capacity to understand themselves in the relationship with their child and in increasing their imaginative and associative capacity – that is, in brief, their capacity to play and to dream unthought, unconscious emotions. The images formed in the field, starting with Elisa's drawing, reached a sort of aesthetic composition at the end of the encounter, as happens when a group of artists dedicate themselves to a shared work of art.

An artistic experience can illustrate what I intend to say, as follows: in 1974, Susan Hiller, an English conceptual artist, involved a group of colleagues in recording their dreams for one month in order to develop a personal form of graphic record of their dreams without making use of a narrative format. During the last three days of the work, the different documents were utilized to collectively draw up the group's map of dreams, which became the representation of the collective dream of the preceding night (see Figures 6.5 and 6.6).

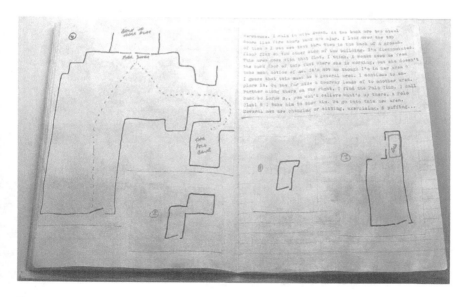

Figure 6.5 Susan Hiller, Dream Mapping, Notebook, 1974

Figure 6.6 Susan Hiller, Dream Mapping, Collective Work, 1974

Notes

1 Brady 2011, Galatzer-Levy 2008, Novick and Novick 2005.
2 Badoni 2002.
3 Chazan 2006.
4 Vallino 2010.
5 Nutella is a chocolate hazelnut spread with a consistency similar to peanut butter.
6 Bonaminio et al. 1989, Otte 1999, Weiss 1995.
7 Fabozzi 2015, Greenberg 1997.
8 Winnicott 1958b.
9 "*I suggest that the mother hates the baby before the baby hates the mother, and before the baby can know his mother hates him*" (Winnicott 1958b, p. 241).
10 Ambrosiano 1998.
11 Ogden 2007, p. 575.
12 Ferro 2005, p. 430.
13 Bleger 1967, Ogden 1989. In Civitarese 2008, the author observed how it is possible to catch emotions in an autistic area of the field in order to theorize one of the specific tools to do so: transformation into hallucinosis. See also Civitarese 2015.
14 Fairbairn 1952.
15 Golberg 1995, Guntrip 1968.
16 Bion 1961, p. 111.
17 Winnicott 1965a, p.182.
18 Neri 2002, p. 392.
19 Kaës 2009, p. 117.
20 Bion 1962b, p. 82. The concept of binocular vision – or "*the need for employing a technique of constantly changing points of view*" (p. 86) – is the third of Bion's ideas of mental functioning. This concept strongly underscores that thought necessarily involves a view of reality from multiple vantage points (or "*vertices*", as Bion called them in Bion 1965, p. 90) and simultaneously. For example: combining the conscious and the unconscious, or the paranoid-schizoid and depressive positions, the psychotic and the non-psychotic parts of the personality.
21 Corrao 1971, p. 9, translated by Gina Atkinson.
22 Bion 1961.
23 Bion 1970.
24 Hellman et al. 1972, p. 323.
25 Corrao 1998.
26 Baranger and Baranger 1961–62, Corrao 1989, Grotstein 2004b, Ferro 2008b.
27 Altman 2002.
28 Frankel 1998, Hopkins 2000, Sugarman 2003.
29 Amir 2010. In this article, the author explores the feature of a living language able to transmit and to process emotions. She highlights the necessity for the analyst to build a language that is in itself an emotional container and an apparatus of meaning. Amir shows how concrete language can be a way for the patient to show to the analyst the place where the emotional truth and the meaning has dwelled. The discovery of meaning for the family of my little patient became possible through the aesthetic experience of the drawings, a symbolic language in which words do not become a filter for emotional truth.

Chapter 7

Sunday cartoons and very young patients

> Being a cartoonist means learning to work with space limitations. The power of cartoons is to succeed in doing a lot with a little. . . . That said, at some point simplification hinders the storytelling.
>
> Bill Watterson[1]

Bill Watterson, the author of *Calvin and Hobbes*, in the introduction to one of his books, talks about the turning point in his work when the newspaper that published his comic strips let him use a half page without any layout restrictions once a week.

The strips published every day had to adjust to a limited space that at times had to be further adapted because of publishing needs. Over time, these limitations made him feel constrained, a feeling that ended up affecting his creative work. Following lengthy negotiations, his editor finally gave him a bigger and free-of-restraints format in the Sunday issue. Watterson realized that in drawing his Sunday cartoons in a larger format he was able not only to have his artwork more respected but also the variations of the cartoon form and their free intermingling allowed for new representations.

Bill Watterson's description of his work inspired me to intuit how the variation of shape or space where the characters act produces a deep modification of representation itself.

In this chapter, I report an analytic experience where something analogous happened: a change of setting brought about a deep transformation in the analytic process and allowed for the development of hypotheses about the possibility that very young children can play a remarkable therapeutic role in specific situations. Their presence can promote the possibility of reaching and disentangling areas where transgenerational ghosts or hard-to-be-reached body memories are embedded.

The birth of the idea

Sara, back from a short break we had agreed upon following the birth of her child, told me that she needed to bring her baby to one of our three weekly sessions. I agreed with pleasure, as I was curious to see the child who had been with us in his mother's womb for nine months and about whom I had fantasized, wondering what his experience of analysis before his birth might have been. I also assumed that my patient had several reasons to have her child in the session: her partial difficulty dealing with separation and the resonance that this difficulty could have in the vicissitudes of my patient and her own analysis. However, I did not imagine that the analysand's request was not concerning only that one session. To my surprise, the following week she came again with her baby, and this new arrangement went on for a few months.

The three-person session was the second of the three weekly sessions, so I started to identify it as the middle session. Part of me wished to understand the meaning of the new arrangement into which I had been partly dragged. Another part was determined to wait for a potential meaning to emerge from that experience and the joint work of our minds.

Whilst in the first encounters after having resumed, the child sat in his baby's chair most of the time, making his presence felt with some wails, and his being there gradually became more present until he took the liberty of being part of our adults' exchange. I had let the young mother sit in the armchair so that holding the baby in her lap would be easier, but switching our positions – hers on the couch and mine behind her – was a disturbing and therefore unacceptable offer.

Starting with these thoughts about the body and my patient's position in the room, we began our reflection. The patient started to reveal the issue, saying that she felt as if her child distracted us so much that she experienced the session as a waste of time and money. It was hard to restructure our space, planned for two, and to make it flexible so as to adjust it to an ever-changing situation. On the other hand, still considering the actual but not insurmountable difficulties in entrusting the baby to somebody's care during the session, I kept wondering why we both – probably for different reasons – wanted him physically there between us.

We continued for a while in a somewhat grotesque situation. The patient lay on the couch, then she would stand up to take the child on her lap, and sometimes the most practical solution was to breastfeed him because after that the sated child would fall asleep lying against her breast. I observed the mother and her child in a position that looked very uncomfortable, and I would end up feeling just as uncomfortable in an armchair all for myself. The traditional setting, that the patient felt as something she just could not give up and held on to it by keeping at least her usual posture, was a limitation in terms of a space that had allowed us to go through many stories and to do a lot with a little for many years. But now, in this situation, it did show some form of constraint.

The three-person session was gradually becoming a 'Sunday' session – that is, a session where the space of our 'orderly little squares' felt disrupted and sometimes seemed as if we were not working. And yet we also shared the feeling that it had become a space in which we could experiment something new.

Alternating 'orderly little squares' and free drawings

Like Bill Watterson, we were proceeding along two registers: we had two classic sessions where we worked within our given 'little squares', and we both felt that the stories could go through a narrative course and some continuity that only that kind of space could afford. Then there was the 'Sunday' session where the internal space of the session was disrupted, and we had to restore its capacity through a psychically more creative action.

The novelty, at least for me, was not so much having a child and her mother in analysis[1] — as a child analyst, I practise mother-and-child treatment, and I am used to observations and interventions, including the active presence of one or both parents — but that they were there without any clear problem in their relationship. The relational difficulty with the infant was to be captured at a different level. The issue of the double register that more evidently regarded the setting of the sessions at some point felt to me as also concerning the kind of dialogue in the three-person sessions. At times, both the mother and I were able to maintain dialogue by putting the child aside, without really excluding him. At other times, the presence of the child attracted our attention, and we were both reaching out to him, making hypotheses about the kind of need he expressed non-verbally that sometimes was concretely met by his mother. When this happened, we both experienced a diversion from the discourse unfolding between the two of us, and that distraction had, for the time being, that negative meaning that school education had instilled in us.

The hypothesis of latent creativity had been validated outside the session as I considered that a mother capable of developing some thoughts *"in brackets"* – that is, capable of keeping in mind her relationship with the child while she is interacting with another subject – allows the child to internalize a safety feeling.[2] It seemed to me that the continuity ensured by the patient with her child while she was talking with me was also a particularly valuable experience for her, as she had gone through dramatic and repeated affective disrupters during her life. The child, being a person in his own right and not only a part of the infantile self, exerted a creative twist on this issue.

The experience of again finding some continuity in discontinuity, that at first was a challenge in alternating different settings, also appeared in the session, and the capacity to manage and integrate verbally and non-verbally what happened implied an effort in a new direction. What seemed to slowly emerge was that, in the three-person sessions, we began to experience some overlapping freedom and emphasis on the value of non-verbal communications and images that were different from the classic sessions.

As in the following comic strips, the session started ordinarily with a narrative, but then it expanded not only in terms of the number of participants – because of the active participation of the child – but also because several fantasies unfolded and supported one another so that, in the end, they would compose a little square of reality (see Figure 7.1).

These fantasies explored in particular prehistoric areas of the field – that is, aspects of the primitive functioning of the mind and the most archaic ways of relating.

In the three-person sessions, the capacity to be surprised and play more boldly was gradually supporting us in our choice not to abandon that strange invention, despite the practical difficulties it seemed to impose on us. When Sara, after some months, was able to stand up from the armchair and the three of us could sit on the mat together, she said that she felt pleasantly well. This new feeling was not stemming from something

Figure 7.1 Sunday cartoon: field's expansion

CALVIN AND HOBBES © 1986, 1992 and 1993 Watterson. Reprinted with permission of UNIVERSAL UCLICK. All rights reserved.

I did or said but from her capacity to play with her infantile self within and without.[3] She recalled a dream from the beginning of her analysis where she and I were eating a sandwich together sitting on the mat – a dream that at that time, in the midst of intense emotional storminess, had seemed a dreamlike relational haven. Since that session, Sara stopped bringing her child to the sessions, as she had reportedly found someone who would take care of the infant during that time.

The experience I have reported here also brought a new perspective in the treatment of very young children with their mothers in situations where the request for analysis comes from serious difficulties in the primary relationship. In the situation with Sara, I had a chance to observe how the non-verbal contribution of the infant introduced in the analytic field some mutative factors that can be grasped only through the use of space, gestures and the non-verbal in general as forms preceding the possibility to explore conscious and unconscious emotions.[4]

In particular, children can concentrate something that in finding its expression with the body collects non-symbolic elements and makes more evident some elements that are difficult to observe in the relationship to the adult. The particular sensitivity of young children can capture relational vibrations of the group field and transform them into signals. To use a comparison, we can imagine them like the soldiers who, in World War I, aboard the early rudimentary submarines, were able to identify the approaching ships by holding a monkey wrench in their mouths: one end between their lips and the other against the metal walls of the submarine. In this way, they could feel the vibrations – that could not be felt through any other sense – with their mouths.[5]

I will illustrate this hypothesis and relate some fragments from the two-person (mother and analyst) and the three-person (mother, analyst and infant) sessions in a pathological situation.

Ordinary strips and Sunday cartoons in a mother-and-child therapy

Anna is a young woman who had a previous analysis where she managed to overcome a severe eating disorder and to contain various types of self-harming behaviour. But giving birth to a baby girl has stirred her deeper and not fully resolved anxieties that translated into violent acts against the child and obsessive behaviour where Anna tries to manage an overwhelming feeling of disintegration. Anna separated from her partner a few months after the birth of the child. At first, the analysand emphasized the oppressive burden she experienced whenever she felt that other people decided for her.

Supported by the experience I have just referred to and Anna's feelings, I suggested we work jointly with her and her child, leaving her the possibility to choose every time whether to come to treatment alone or with her daughter. For her to become active in managing the setting, understood as the body of analysis, as a place where the least thinkable anxieties can be deposited, seemed to return to her some form of competence about her own needs and show that the setting could constitute an active ingredient of therapy for *"patients too scared to think"*.[6]

I will describe, through some fragments of two- and three-person sessions, how their intertwining helped us explore various areas of the field.

A two-person session

Anna arrives without her daughter, Laura. As soon as she comes in, she tells me that she had a nightmare last night: she dreamed of a big spider that slipped into Laura's bed. Since Anna could not see the insect, her anxiety grew out of proportion, and she woke up drenched in sweat.

She tells me that spiders, especially the hairy ones, are not just a phobia for her but a source of real terror, so that following her daughter's birth, she has slept for months wearing her glasses to be able to see any spider in case she had to get up during the night. She says that she has tried several remedies to keep the spiders out of the house: she sprayed chlorine on the doorposts, she vacuumed systematically in every corner of the house, engaged in an uneven and losing struggle as the spiders continued to sneak in through the old walls. Then she adds, with a shy and triumphant smile, that the only way to stop them effectively when she saw them on the walls was to spray them with hair lacquer.

The image of lacquered spiders reminds me of a semi-magic effect of a paralyzing fluid that allows her not to lose sight of the enemy without killing it. This latter event would expose Anna to uncontrollable guilt feelings.

Spiders are what she cannot master, horror-and-fear laden, the familiar that causes disgust without expecting that. Watterson represents this aspect about the familiar turning into persecutory when he transforms Hobbes, the faithful stuffed tiger friend, into a treacherous animal that can suddenly attack Calvin or show that the objects Calvin cannot master, such as the bicycle, become objects that can actively attack (see Figure 7.2).

The spiders contain everything Anna is terrified of: her own smallness, her daughter's smallness, sexuality and the nameless dread elicited by the emotions she cannot work through. I imagine that they are also the carriers of her fear about our sessions when she is alone with me and is afraid I could say something painful that cannot be handled. Even when she is here with her daughter, she feels observed and fears being judged, but it is as if her focus on the child preserves her from this persecutory anxiety, at least in part.

The sessions are demanding for me because, as Anna said, we can move analytically only if we stay still: a difficult paradox to experience. I try to navigate between these opposites and tell her that the lacquered spiders are an artistic solution. I say that Louise Bourgeois[7] did something similar with steel and that she, too, with her sculptures, tried to put together her

Sunday cartoons and very young patients 117

Figure 7.2 Daily strip: persecutory object
CALVIN AND HOBBES © 1986, 1992 and 1993 Watterson. Reprinted with permission of UNIVERSAL UCLICK. All rights reserved.

love for her mother and the feeling of aggressiveness and entrapment that this relationship created for her. Through her sculptures, she created a feeling of safety that she had never before experienced.

When I say 'mother', I obviously include myself, as I am aware that I am also dangerous. But I do not know how we can create a form in this space that can allow us to generate a feeling of safety enabling us to deal with the transformation of emotions that are now dangerously evacuated with aggressive acts against the child – the subject embodying helplessness.

Anna responds to my words about the sculptures by recalling how she scribbled on the wall when she was a child and then turned her scribbles into little spiders, adding six legs. Her mother hit her, but she stubbornly kept on doing it. Through this memory, Anna seems to get in touch with both a nascent symbolic capacity to create images and an old thrust to be herself in a defiant attitude. This first form of containment and transformation that Anna is able to provide to herself reminds me of a detail I found in a book where the architectonic intelligence of animals is described. In particular, I remember that a certain type of wasps build their cells and seal them with a peculiar store of food for the growing larvae.

They paralyze a spider with their poison and place it at the extremity of the cell so that the spider is alive but cannot escape. I tell Anna about this thought, but after the session, I think that the reverie that developed in my mind in fact condenses in one image several conscious and unconscious emotional elements in the field: persecutory anxiety is combined with the attempted construction of a containing function, the paralyzing poisonousness of some emotions can also become food for thought through the development of transformative functions.

So, we have a script written together with pictures moving as follows: a spider slips into a crib (a persecutory aspect and a helpless character) → a lacquered spider (the defence) → a gigantic spider (the persecution becomes hyperbolical but at the same time is combined with an artistic form) → a tiny spider drawn on the wall (a nascent creative aspect in Anna) → a living yet immobile spider that has become food for larvae (a troubling image that condenses an expectation of birth with an image of lethal paralysis at the end of the session).

This is the greatest transformation we manage to put in place in this session with the two of us.

To go back to the analogy with the cartoons, we can see in Figure 7.3 how the maternal unavailability, or the relative capacity of the analyst to accept and transform intolerable emotions, can appear in a narrative process that produces some evolution but brings about the working through of some emotions to some extent which still has the features of entrapment.

Figure 7.3 Sunday cartoon: analyst's unavailability

CALVIN AND HOBBES © 1986, 1992 and 1993 Watterson. Reprinted with permission of UNIVERSAL UCLICK. All rights reserved.

The following three-person session

To change rooms depending on Anna coming alone or with her child seemed to be too disruptive, so I decided to stay in the consulting room where I work with adult patients and just to change the way we would use it.

When I am only with her, we work in a vis-a-vis setting; when the child is also with us, we sit on the mat where I arrange some cushions and a few toys. Anna starts the session with her child and me by describing how anxious she feels because of the weaning process, as she is sure that some food causes constipation. But since, in her imagination, these staples change over time, she has gradually tried to eliminate all the ingredients, so that now she is feeding her child only with very basic food. This trial has led her to go through several conflicts that have expanded like a blaze: first with the father who she contacts now and then and who reflects her craziness back to her, then with the child who wishes to taste the food she sees on the table but is prevented from doing so and finally with the paediatrician with whom she quarrelled violently this morning.

I think that Anna, in her narrative, is sharing with us how keeping the waste inside is anxiety provoking because she knows the upsetting experience of violent evacuation. Her wish for a simple, easy-to-digest diet that does not cause any difficulty is what she wishes from her treatment, too. But I also think of the image that came to my mind at the end of last session: the larvae fed with paralyzed spiders seem to be somehow connected with Anna's wish to oversimplify the food for her child. This association allows me to listen more trustfully as the process is unfolding. The father's and the paediatrician's words – full of good intentions and healthy sensibility, although expressed in a very judgemental way – seem to be very far from contacting Anna's anxiety and are also a valuable indication for me.

Anna swings between the need for regression and merging and the wish for tasty food that implies the ability to break it down, chew and incorporate it and finally evacuate the waste. She feels she is lacking all these functions.

Anna resumes her account and says that she managed to find a babysitter who could take care of the child for a few hours. She did not leave home, but she took advantage of that time to have a shower. She has observed her child and the babysitter surreptitiously as they were playing with the dog, and again she felt overwhelmed by anxiety-ridden thoughts. She thought about the possibility that the dog could bite the child and bring filth into the house with her daughter possibly becoming seriously ill.

I comment that it is really difficult to decide what is good and what is bad. I opt for this minimal, almost tasteless interpretative style, similar to the food she cooks for her child. I think that Anna is telling me about her wish to live as a separate being, but the anxiety stirred by that condition ends up backfiring: her beloved dog becomes a dangerous carrier of infection and suddenly the familiar becomes a source of persecution.

In the meanwhile, the child, who has been playing with the toys, looks around and starts to crawl towards a low piece of furniture with some objects on its top. They are my objects, which I have collected over the years as affective and symbolic representations of my being a psychoanalyst, and I think I am not happy at all about the turn the situation is now taking.

The child holds on to the furniture, stands up and reaches out her little hands to take a wooden statue; from all the objects, this is the least bad, and I keep quiet. Then she puts the head of the statue in her mouth, and her saliva starts to run over my beloved statue. Anna does not look worried at all, whereas I feel like those people living at the foot of the volcano during an eruption.

Anna is stroking her child, who enjoys the right softness/hardness of the wooden head of the statue into which she is sinking her sharp little teeth.

Now I am housing the immobility of the spider with its persecutory derivatives. Part of me is bitten and damaged, and I am not comfortable at all. In spite of this, I cannot express aloud or with any gesture my will to preserve my objects.

Anna: 'I need to go back to work, and I do not like that job'. (Anna teaches in a high school.) They are not bad kids, but they do not understand anything. Many of them have incredibly tough backgrounds.

She has changed the subject, and I try to tie all the different threads together again, which entails the management of emotions that do not belong only to Anna now but pervade the interplay field.

Faced with my temporary paralysis, Anna seems rather to follow the flow of saliva from her child's mouth and tells me something more, leaving aside the constipation issue that often takes up much of the session. She is talking about what she dislikes in relationships.

I comment that, in working with students, not everyone can see the link between their difficult life histories, their odd behaviour and their learning difficulties.

In the meantime, the child drops the statue on the floor and gets hold of a puppet I have prepared on the mat, a big stuffed mouse. I wonder whether she is following us in her own way (dropping an object/a discourse to grasp a different one) or if she is preceding us. In which case, where is she taking us? Maybe more concretely inside emotional sewers?

Anna resumes talking and says that last year one of her students gave her an essay asking for her opinion. Anna thought that it was a delusional diary, but not to offend him and to help him understand that she appreciated his trust, she tried to highlight the weaknesses and strengths in his writing.

He replied, 'Do you believe me when I tell you that I could staple one of my ears?' And even before getting a reply, he rushed to the stapler and pierced his ear, with blood spurting everywhere and staining the surroundings.

Two things strike me: the self-harming gesture and realizing that I also have just made an appreciation about her. It is as if Anna underscores that, while I highlight her capable and sensitive parts, she is here because she needs me to help her understand her crazy acts. Stapling, or in my imagination cutting off her ear, seems to embody the indication of not wanting or not being able to handle any criticisms.

At this point, the child wants to tear off the tail of the mouse and starts to whine angrily. Anna intervenes abruptly with rage, as if the girl has distracted us from her painful discourse. Worried about the potential violent gestures that she sometimes exhibits with her child, I intervene hastily.

I say, 'You see, the issue – you were talking about – stuck to me and, like at the cinema when I watch a scary scene, I look elsewhere. When you were talking about your student, I thought of van Gogh's cut-off ear and the horror and the blood . . . and so I got distracted and looked at your daughter'.

I do not think it is just about distraction because I try to trust the polyphonic composition of the group, and I think that the child participates actively in what is going on, but it is emotionally true that I wished for the scene to change. I imagine that through the very impossibility of separating the mouse from its tail, the child is bringing us back to the topic of being trapped.

Anna sighs, 'Yes, the blood'.

We are in an atmosphere full of blood, pain and madness. As we do not speak, the child shifts from whining to crying. I think again about the lacquered spiders and then the huge spiders, and it seems to me that the disproportionate growth of some emotions linked to the sensation of being trapped is again between us, recreated through the images that the three of us have built together.

Anna comforts her child, who starts to explore the room again. She picks up the stuffed mouse and gets interested in the label that all toys have as a certification of the materials. She looks at it, manipulates and tastes it. Anna comments that she is also careful in buying toys made with safe materials. She smiles at her daughter and at me.

We talk about toys and how they can be a tool of creativity and a poison at the same time. I wonder what the labels could represent, and I think that Laura might have picked up my anxiety when I was afraid of her mother's aggressiveness.

I say that a grandmother I know made a strange toy for her grandchild by sticking many labels on a ribbon.

Anna is a very sharp woman, and I did not need to make it any more explicit. The session ends up with this image of something not toxic that can be bought and transformed into a toy.

Praise of the turning point produced by the child

More than once, in this alternating setting with two or three participants, I have experienced the unconscious contribution of the child, but at first – as I could not recognize any dignity of thought in what happened – I just thought it was accidental.

When the resistance against what is brought by the novelty faded away, my curiosity paved the way to reflection. Bill Watterson played a role in this process.

In the two-person session, our minds produced narratives and images that followed and affected one another just as in comic strips. The images have their own internal consistency and trace a plot about the underlying emotional processing. Let us follow the spider's vicissitudes:

IMAGE	EMOTION
A spider sneaking into the crib	Danger and helplessness
A lacquered spider	Mastering helplessness by recruiting defences
A gigantic steel spider	The emotion has become hyperbolical
A small spider drawn on the wall	A creative mixture of the ability to reduce exaggeration and the beginning of representation
A living spider but motionless food for larvae	An image of life and deadly helplessness at the same time

In the three-person session, the child's presence through her action and body introduces a less orderly and more surprising form in the narrative by pictures that are created in the field.

When the child bites the statue, I do not think about the discomfort of being assaulted, but in my body, I feel the uncomfortable experience of helplessness. In hindsight, I think that Laura, in biting the statue's head, expressed something of her own experience when her mother becomes mad and unconsciously communicated to me some emotions that accompany such an experience. To feel that something of oneself is irreparably damaged drives to some common sharing where helplessness drives me being an analyst towards a less controlled way of relating where the other is needed.

IMAGE	EMOTION
Simple food	Desire for food that can be digested and does not create difficulties in waste disposal
Dog	The return of persecutory anxiety allows her to intuit that some defences are not effective
The bitten head	Violent aspect that is difficult to grasp emotionally
The wounded ear	The body as a container of the evacuated emotions; enacted and suffered violence
The big mouse with the tail that does not come off	The ongoing expression of being trapped
The label of non-toxic materials	The beginning of a dialogue about the initial theme of the session so that emotions can be transformed

As we go over the succession of images and characters and the emotions they convey, we capture more clearly the contribution of the child (in bold type).

Although from different perspectives, many authors agree that the child is an active subject in family analytic therapy.[8] In some cases, the child not only is active in a general sense but also is able to introduce powerful elements of healing in the intersubjective field.[9] For example, some drawings may contain elements that can monitor the group unconscious, including the analyst's unconscious. The symbolic contribution of children can be used in the relationship with the parents, not so much to communicate to them something regarding the child's treatment but as a facilitator of therapy that the analyst can activate with the whole family.

In the experience I have described here, I have assumed that even very young children who cannot bring to the analytic field any symbolic production can in fact play an important and actively therapeutic role in the mutative process of unconscious emotions.

Being three in the session has some bending effect that transforms what Ogden calls the analytic third, an area in which things are created as the process unfolds without being able to distinguish what belongs to one or the other.[10] The analytic third is the product of the unconscious exchange of the two subjects of analysis in a dialectic tension and ongoing evolution.

In a way, we could say that the child can embody something of the internal process of the analytic third and make an active contribution to its evolution to O – that is, to what is not yet known.[11]

The young child, in this three-person setting, introduces a variation of the pace of verbal exchanges in the relationship between the adults and creates some openings for concrete body interaction. The experience that the child imposes brings a noticeable element of unexpectability if compared to the one we experience in verbal dialogue. At first, that unexpectable dimension is perceived as a sometimes annoying distraction from one's thoughts or words. As in the cartoon, the expectation of conversation as a safe place where one can experiment oneself may suddenly disappear under the burden of an action that upsets, attacks and makes emotions more overwhelming (see Figure 7.4).

Figure 7.4 Sunday cartoon: an unexpected event
CALVIN AND HOBBES © 1986, 1992 and 1993 Watterson. Reprinted with permission of UNIVERSAL UCLICK. All rights reserved.

The response is to look around, seeking an opportunity, something that can contain the lack of safe ground to stand on. Time expands, and the thought of a session that can be catastrophically useless sneaks into the mind of one of the participants.

Although for a long while, I considered the distraction as a negative element; later, I became aware of its value, starting with its creative role in development. Adults often identify children's distraction as a difficulty linked to their functional immaturity in keeping their attention for a long time. Considering distraction in these terms is like stating that a child's drawing is wrong because it is full of mistakes, if we view visual realism as the only goal of cognitive maturation. Just as the mistakes of perspective or proportions are the real artistic ingredient of a child's drawing, distraction is an important creative developmental element.

Since the beginning of the relationship, the apparent disappearance of the child in the interactive exchanges with the mother has played a key role akin to the importance of the times of intense relational exchange.[12] The inability in some mothers to respect these moments of distraction in the child creates a paradoxical response that stirs disorienting anxieties that damage the development of thinking.[13]

With older children, it is also a common experience that, when reading or playing, they are drawn by something else and turn their eyes somewhere else, sometimes moving the whole body to become engaged in another experience. While this can mortify the parents at times, in fact it signals curiosity that becomes disciplined slowly over time, if it is respected.

As adults, a trace of this kind of shifting from one thing to another can be found mostly in thinking. The psychoanalytic method emphasizes this characteristic, as it considers free association a creative pillar in thinking.

In the sessions with very young children, we might call this process free dissociation, a method that, starting with freely floating attention, expands the catastrophic experiential aspects so as to recompose them creatively.

The gesture that can make the emotion hyperbolical stems from the children's peculiar sensitivity and receptivity of unconscious emotions in the field.

Daily and Sunday strips

In working with children and their families, we experience how any variation of the external setting corresponds to a variation of the analyst's internal setting. The more the former moves away from the classic setting, the more necessary it is for the internal setting to be sound. But sound does not mean rigid. Sound describes the chance to do or to think without internally losing the capacity to keep alive inside oneself the possibility of making analytic sense of what is happening.

To accept a changing setting – so as to follow the possibility for the patient together with the analyst, to build a space-time apt to give shape to the patient's own experience – has allowed us to go through an experience where the experimental arrangement of the setting affected the process deeply.

The setting has become a stage capable of affecting the emotional development of the analytic story and the bond between the subjects, just as with Bill Watterson when he started to draw in a bigger and less organized space in the Sunday edition.

At first, the possibility to maintain a dialogue on a double track in the sessions was a relational arrangement that replicated in the analytic setting something that happens in the family when the adults exclude or include the child and still maintain psychic continuity and group link. So, I had hypothesized that I could carry out a mother-child analysis in the three-person sessions and a classic analysis in the two-person sessions. The absence of the child in the latter stirred my curiosity about any difference in our dialogue with respect to the child's virtual or actual presence.

I realized that the bodily presence of the child deeply changed how the session would unfold, our way of interacting and the atmosphere we were immersed in.

Initially, I could see how the 'little square sessions' – that is, our sessions in the classic setting – allowed us to explore some areas of our shared intersubjective field, whilst in the three-person sessions, other areas of the field would let fantasies, deeper and more involving potentials and anxieties, emerge because of the variation of the form.

In other words, the three-person sessions can bring back into the experience and therefore into the thinking process something that cannot always find a home in the two-person sessions. In the three-person sessions, the therapist is forced to be slightly off centre and to go through a more noticeable emotional oscillation, where emotional attunement is more complex. In the three-person sessions, similar to what happens in group therapy, there are two levels of fantasies: a more explicit level that evolves through verbal and non-verbal interplay – what Bion calls evolution in K – and a level made of formless fantasies. The latter cannot be known directly but can evolve in what Bion called evolution in O – that is, what is unknown. At this latter level, the child brings his specific contribution by introducing a more meaningful bodily and sensory component and his body in action. This, in particular, has a disorganizing and reorganizing effect on the analytic work that is functionally more effective than the regularity of a mostly narrative process.

The child's acting, to my view, drives every member of the group to intensify the fantasies that remain formless for some time in the field. This emotional agglomerate that is mobile and enriched by every single subject cannot be known directly, but it can evolve and find a body expression again in the child, the subject in the group who has naturally greater expressive sensitivity about the form of sensations and unconscious emotions.

Paradoxically, in the three-person sessions, it is not the narrative that lets scattered emotions or emotions felt as mere tension by the other participants emerge but the child's bodily action, whose contribution is essential to work through those very emotions.[14]

Notes

1 *Calvin and Hobbes: Sunday Pages 1985–1995* © 2001 Bill Watterson (Andrews McMeel Publishing). Reprinted with kind permission.
2 Alvarez 2012.
3 Bloom 2000.
4 Stern 1988, Norman 2001, Salomonsson 2007, Beebe 2014.
5 Haim Baharrier, La Genesi spiegata da mia figlia [Genesis explained by my daughter], Milano: Garzanti, 2006. The girl, explaining the Bible to her father, named in the title, is affected by Down syndrome. The book, and my understanding of the book, wants to highlight how the cognitive deficit sometimes improves the sensorial communicative abilities that are as effective as words.
6 Winnicott has pointed out the importance of setting with borderline patients. Tuch has confirmed these hypothesis in his research (Tuch 2007, 2011; Winnicott 1958a).
7 Bourgeois 2007.
8 Lyons-Ruth 1999, Rocha Barros 2000, Salo 2007.
9 Molinari 2013a and now the previous chapter.
10 Ogden 2004c.
11 Bion 1970, Grotstein 2004a.
12 Beebe and Lachmann 2002, Stern 1985, Winnicott 1941.
13 Di Ceglie 2013.
14 Corrao 1992, Neri 2007.

Chapter 8

Action across emptiness

Nik Wallenda is an acrobat known as the first person to have walked across the Grand Canyon on a tightrope without a safety net or harness. For this man, walking across emptiness is a challenge which – as he says in interviews – makes him feel part of the tradition of his family, a family of high-wire walkers. In the video featuring his performance, you can see him walk slowly and keep his balance with a balancing pole whereby he counters the wire's oscillations and the air currents. When the challenge becomes excessive, you see how he deals with the danger: he squats on the tightrope and then thanks God who has helped him stop the wire from swinging. To withstand and negotiate the oscillation seems to him the key factor for survival. His family and his faith are the keys to how he copes with anxiety. In 2013, Wallenda collected his experiences in a memoir titled *Balance*.[1]

I was strongly impressed by Nik Wallenda's filmed performance, and the word *balance* led me to consider how keeping balance is functional not only for physical but also for psychic survival. The child, in order to be born mentally, needs to acquire the ability to swing between different psychic states. Two elements seem to be necessary for this venture: developing a creative capacity that transforms emptiness into a relationship with the other and being confident that the other can help. If this happens, then the size of the emotional oscillation becomes acceptable, and the mind learns how to keep its balance, navigate the disturbances and trust the bond. When developing normally, the child organizes the space between his mother and himself in an adaptive and rhythmical interaction by alternating separateness and merging. That space is populated with abstractions, models and containers for the sensations that are produced by early experiences. The innate forms – that is, the abstract, aesthetic, geometric, musical forms of rhythm – organize the early relational experiences and become the essential element from which thinking and feeling develop.[2] The intrapsychic regulation of the tension originates from rhythm – a bridge between the body and the mind – and the capacity to wait develops. From that comes the trust in the other-outside-oneself and the hope to be supported.

But if the capacity to hallucinate the breast, and then to represent it, does not develop from these early forms, or if outside help is ineffective, then instead of the breast there is not an empty space but nothingness mixed with unmanageable anxiety. Disoriented in the face of the abyss, the child clings to an aberrant sensory dimension and to objects that seem to be reliable and unchangeable because of their concrete nature. Disconnecting from the mother turns into a chasm, and using objects and forms creates a prison from which it is increasingly difficult to escape. A sensation of annihilation, similar to breaking down into catastrophic anxiety, prevails and turns into extreme relational withdrawal and difficulty in managing the ensuing sensations and emotions.

Imagining walking on a tightrope over an abyss without a safety net may allow us to intuit the degree of anxiety aroused in some patients when confronted with relating to others. It may also explain why it takes a long time in treatment to create and strengthen the prerequisites to develop the ability to manage emotional oscillations.

In treating patients who use massive forms of proto-containment – that is to say, a non-psychic way of navigating the experience – the analyst shares particular kinds of sensations and emotions helpful for the evolution of the process and a different state that prompts retreat into a relational withdrawal similar to the patient's. Here, I would like to focus on a blockage of the psychic tension – ensuring vital oscillations – between plunging into the forms of the patient's psychic existence and surfacing from these forms so as to become more aware of how to handle this difficulty in order to progress slowly along the therapeutic process with the patient. In particular, I will explore a form of interaction that originated from this kind of oscillation and allowed me to stretch a tightrope across the emptiness between a child with autistic traits in therapy and myself so that we could bridge that gap step by step.

A potential extension of the concept of oscillation at the origin of psychic birth

Much of an autistic child's difficulty comes from the lack of an apparatus to work through emotions that originate in the relationship. Withdrawal, as an extreme defence, is a kind of sensory self-containment unwilling to make use of the other. Bion says that in the healthy infant – healthy in terms of pre- and postnatal psycho and physical atonement – at some point in his early development "*a state of expectation*"[3] of a capacity of containment outside the infant himself may arise, some kind of innate *preconception* of being contained. This hypothesis suggests that initially all infants can also be inhabited by a fantasy of self-containment as well as by the preconception of relational containment. Self-containment would then occur through a proto-container formed of some kind of β elements – that Bion identifies as "*row*"[4] – that are not associated with the need to expel intolerable sensations or emotions. These kinds of β elements are not the product of the transformative failure of a function and therefore are not expelled from the psyche as units of experience that cannot be transformed. They create a kind of sensory and affective contour which emerges from the flow of physical exchanges between two interacting subjects, register the form of the objects through a mimetic function and act as precursors of an actual containment function.[5] They thus form a primary unit of experience, an area of the mind where sensory and mental experiences remain indistinct.[6] Besides this early form of containment, the preconception of an external containment promotes the experience of projection of raw emotions (β elements) in space. If β elements find a transformation in the mother's mind, then they can be re-introjected and used to develop dreaming and thinking. Therefore, we can suppose that at the beginning of development there are two functions to contain and transform the emotions and sensations. Both functions develop on two different levels. On one level, containment is formed through a mimetic process, a flow of adhesive forms of identification where the primitive fantasy is to adhere to the object, its shape and to spatial density, whereas, on the transformative level, the transformation of sensory experience is turned into forms of signification through α function. If development unfolds seamlessly, the β proto-container continues to work in a subordinate position to ♀/♂ functioning and maintains the function of hosting aspects of the merging experience in ♀/♂ oscillation similar to PS-D oscillation. In a developmental perspective, we can assume that the development of the actual ♀/♂ function is activated only in relation to the function necessary for sensory recognition, for which the proto-container has greater specificity and sensitivity. Mimetic recognition creates a feeling of trust and activates ♀/♂ function and, in particular, a remote functioning such as projection and introjection. The proto-container could play, on a psychic level, a function similar to the one played by the low amount of dendritic cells in the tissue and mucosa of the immune system when coming into contact with the outside environment. Dendritic cells are particularly sensitive to the stereoscopic recognition of non-self antigens and can link them firmly. This linking activates them and promotes their migration into the lymphoid tissue. Here, they interact with the immune cells to initiate the configuration of the actual immune response.

So, we can imagine that the proto-container and the container are functionally designed to cooperate in learning and regulating the sensory/emotional response. The development of ♀/♂ function implies the ability to project β elements. This ability seems to develop through the activation of a specific site for introjection and projection through the combination of an antigen for sensory recognition. In the case of people with forms of autistic withdrawal, we can assume that a gap between the functioning of the proto-container and the ♀/♂ function develops at a very early phase of development.

The F factor in relation to the development of ♀/♂ function

In early mother-child interactions, we see some sort of maternal submission with respect to the infant. It is a regression to a form of sensory atonement. Pregnancy prepares the mother for it. When the mother adheres to the infant, in a way that Winnicott calls the *"normal illness of primary maternal preoccupation"*,[7] she protects the child from the traumatic dimension of the real world and lays the foundations for trusting the other-than-oneself. This kind of relationship prompts basic trust in the infant, and the repetition of sensory and emotional atonement experiences makes trust develop into a lasting feeling that becomes hope.[8] We can assume that the feeling of trustful surrender allows for the beginning of the projective and introjective function, an essential factor in ♀/♂ development. In the child where this trust cannot develop, the oscillation between forms of proto-containment and containment consolidates withdrawal, and sensory stimulation prevails. In the treatment of children or adults with autistic traits, the analyst needs to share these early developmental stages with the patient. Like the mother, the therapist also feels submitted to the child, although the massive use of sensory dimension, repetition and adhesive identification are more difficult to tolerate compared to what happens at the beginning of life. In pathological adhesion, the analyst may experience feelings of being smothered and of intrusion.[9]

Thinking about the difference between submission and surrender was particularly helpful to me to understand how this affective aspect can play a key role in the therapeutic relationship and to assume that it also plays a role in the transition where the sensory relationship and the actual function of containment relate to each other. In submitting to the rituality that the infant imposes, one feels like a puppet in the hands of the other, and painful sensations of despondency and withdrawal are experienced. Surrendering is a very different experience from submitting: it is something that happens *"in the presence of the other"* without any clear intentionality, and it leads the person to experience a feeling of acceptance and availability to what is new.[10] In the therapeutic relationship with the autistic child, the analyst needs to go over and through a conglomeration of experiences that belong to both subjects. If the analyst succeeds in changing the experience of submission into a feeling of trusting surrender, then this introduces something that fosters transformation into the field.

This kind of transformation can occur through a complex of therapeutic factors; one of these could be a function that Bion[11] called the F factor. It means being able to trust the perceptions that emerge in the mind and in the body of the analyst concerning the feelings of confusion and submission that characterize the interconnection of the two subjects of the analysis. To introduce into the field some actions that convey the F factor would play a role in promoting the oscillation between sensory atonement – mediated by forms of proto-containment – and the actual function of containment, by activating the projective and introjective function.

The performance: a form of interaction to foster oscillation in the analyst and the child

In the psychoanalytic treatment of an autistic patient, the therapist goes through experiences in which he risks becoming mired.[12] To work through the feeling of being bullied and to transform it into a feeling of trusting surrender – with the consequent introduction of the F factor in the field – is the first step of the transformative process. This first emotional transformation in the therapist then needs to become something that can reach the patient. As autism is a wordless illness that *"needs to be treated without words"*,[13] this transformative movement needs to be expressed through action.

In my clinical experience, which has given rise to these thoughts, I found the action which was the expression of my dawning feeling of trust to resemble an art performance. Performance is a form of art that implies the active involvement of the audience, and the relationship with viewers is not established by the object but by the artist's body itself. Unlike artists who perform in front of an audience, such as dancers or actors, the art performer does not know the final outcome of his interaction, as it is open to the unpredictable contribution of the audience. In a performance, it is the body that conveys emotions and meanings in an unstable balance between the creative intuition at the base of the art piece and the unpredictable response of the audience that makes the artwork concrete. Art performers have a very special relationship with the audience and need to practise the possibility of surrendering in the presence of the other, integrating the other in their minds and actions without being overwhelmed. The performance does not aim to fill the gap by means of an object loaded with meaning but opens up the possibility of keeping an empty space where the contribution of the spectators creates a link that crosses it.

Yoko Ono's *Cut Piece* performance is emblematic in this sense. The artist comes on stage with a pair of scissors by her side. The audience is invited to come up on to the stage, one at a time, and cut a portion of her clothing until the artist ends up almost naked. This is a performance that enacts a very troubling kind of relationship and arouses feelings of loss, anxiety and danger. With autistic patients, we sometimes experience the feeling of being exposed to progressively giving up on our own thoughts which, like our clothes, protect us from excessive self-exposure in order to keep ourselves in balance between trust and submission.[14]

Giulio

Giulio was referred to me when he was four years old, and we started therapy three times a week. The preschool staff had identified some learning difficulties associated with a marked relational withdrawal. The loss of his father in a car accident before his birth seemed to be a traumatic concomitant cause of his relational difficulty.[15] To deal with a severe, long-lasting depression following the accident after Giulio's birth, his mother developed a strong religious faith with hallucinatory nuances that led her to talk to Giulio about his father as though he were alive and present. In his mother's intention, this virtual presence should have been reassuring for the child, but in fact it created an anxiety-ridden ghost that was always present to the boy. The implication of this kind of difficulty is that mother and child live in a symbiotic relationship that thwarts their evolution. In particular, I think that the environmental situation may have accentuated Giulio's constitutional fragility.

I worked with the child and his mother together and individually for the whole period of analysis, adapting the setting many times during the treatment in relation to what I thought were their needs at different times. I do not think that the mother's emotional difficulties were the cause of Giulio's psychic difficulties, but I was sure that overcoming the pain for the loss of her husband would make the mother an active player in caring for her child. In the complexity of this analytical treatment, I shall identify a few sequences where Giulio used repetition stereotypically and defensively to illustrate how we learned to cooperate and emerge from some situations where we were stuck.

Obsessive repetition

For about one year, Giulio would scribble a lot during the sessions. He would work quietly, at times quickly, at times as if he were lost in a maze. When he finished filling one piece of paper, he took another one and resumed his scribbling. During the many months when I was confronted with only this form of interaction, I imagined a variety of things and tried different interventions. At first, I focused on the interaction with the piece of paper to which Giulio was giving his full attention. I was cut off from his visual and auditory fields, and I felt that I did not exist. I would sit next to him and comment aloud how his scribbles filled the entire blank sheet. I would make short remarks about how the pencil produced different sensations associated with how much he pressed or how quickly he drew. The marks of different thickness and how fast he drew the tangled scribbles led me to make some hypotheses on how Giulio had experienced contact and how this took place between us in the session. Sometimes his fast scribbles seemed to create a hypnotic vortex that was functional to protect himself from having a space-time where to exist.

In the first period of analysis, the only tolerable relationship for him was the imitative one. Giulio accepted me putting a piece of paper next to his and just mirroring what he drew. The repetitions to which Giulio resorted disguised his inability to have a psychic emotional containment and showed me his incapacity to symbolize, masking it with a protective yet deadly auto-sensory stimulation. The marks on the sheet were simple scribbles, until the day when Giulio stated that he had just drawn the wire. From that moment onwards, that image went with some odd behaviour, such as lying on the floor for a long time and having fits of extreme agitation, as if he had had an electric shock.

The image of the wire cast some light onto the pitch darkness that inhabited me. Gradually, the wires became his passion in reality as well and not only in his drawings. He began to follow the wires along the walls and became excited when they crossed and intertwined under my desk or near a power strip.

Making sense of Giulio's scribbles revitalized me, and I started to tell him how wires link things together and how these things can become bright, attractive and alive through the electricity carried by the wires. I imagined that being able to activate the object was the most important purpose for a child who had been so unlucky to be born after an event that had created an unbridgeable gap.

Giulio did not seem to be affected by my thoughts and kept on being very tyrannical with me. He imposed on me a script where he became despondent at the slightest variation. His despair translated into aimless hyperactivity or compulsive scribbles. In addition to drawing, turning the light or the taps on and off and opening and closing the doors were the activities that Giulio liked to do in the session. Reiteration did not aim to activate the other, and I could not bridge the gap between us by creating a wire of living electricity.[16] I shared the despair I felt was coming from the impossibility to transform reality with his mother, since Giulio seemed to be making very little progress.

His first performance: from repetition to the unrepeatable

In its Latin etymology, the verb *"to repeat"* means *"to direct oneself to somebody again"*.[17] To repeat refers to a space to go through so as to meet somebody, leaving room for the thought that – regardless of potential failure – we are inhabited by a reasonable hope of success if we try again. In its older meaning, *"to repeat"*, rather than a speech operation as we usually mean it, seems to refer to a body experience, like the child's one where space is what first separates him from his mother's arms.

Learning how to fill that gap is an ability that the child learns through many attempts. It allows the child to go across a physical space as well as the potentially anxiety-generating emptiness that separates him from the other. The experience of repetition in the relationship with an autistic child is different. The first emotion that can pervade the field is hopelessness generated by not being able to meet. Then space resembles more the experience of an extremely distressing emptiness.[18] There is no space that defines the self, there is no external space to cross, and the ensuing hopelessness is clearly shared between patient and analyst.

One day, I was in the bathroom looking dejectedly at the water that Giulio took from the sink and poured from one container to another. He was deaf and impermeable to my interventions. I felt frustrated and unable to move with my mind. I sat on the edge of the bathtub, and I felt the growing desire to sink into passivity, mixed with painful powerlessness. As he went on pouring, some water dropped on the base unit supporting the sink. After a while, Giulio poured out some more water intentionally, then he suddenly poured a whole glass of water on the floor. It was almost summer and, maybe driven by some marine fantasies, unintentionally I stepped into the puddle. Giulio imitated me and we stepped together in the water, dragging it around even outside the bathroom. At the end of the session, our footprints were scattered everywhere and our clothes were quite wet.

When his mother arrived to fetch him, I could see her bewilderment at seeing the surroundings and us in such conditions. I tried to make my foolishness less evident by rustling up some explanation: we had made up a new game.

As I was drying up the floor after the session, I realized that we had in fact scribbled with our feet. This child, who never dared to express a living emotion, tried to pour the water out into a space that he had experienced as being empty, as if he were finally trusting that somebody could do something with it.

In the sequence of pouring the water from glass to glass, Giulio at first enacted what we had already experienced many times with his scribbles. The water that disappeared from one glass reappeared in the other one in an endless flow. It was like turning around to create some kind of perfect mirroring by excluding all disruptive otherness. When I entered the puddle, something in Giulio's functioning was hooked, and I could get some hint at a relational development. Having produced a form, in a way that involved the matter, led me to associate our water-mixed-with-dust dripping with one of Pollock's art pieces.

Action across emptiness

Having produced a form in a way that involved the matter led me to associate our water dripping with one of Pollock's paintings titled *Full Fathom Five*. This title was inspired by the verse – in Shakespeare's *The Tempest* – that Ariel utters to indicate the place where a corpse might lie: in the deep ocean, "*at full fathom five*". In the painting, besides a criss-cross of spiral shapes, one can see a variety of half-destroyed daily objects hidden behind a thick layer of paint: bottle caps, clips, cigarettes. During the restoration using X-rays, a human figure appeared at the bottom of the painting – as if the artist had buried the figure there. Pollock looked for an inclusive relationship through his paintings. He said that he painted on the floor so as to feel part of the painting itself.

Thus, we can imagine that the human figure lying on the canvas is the painter himself – or rather a mortified part of himself that was buried in the depth of his art. This story crossed my mind shortly after the performance that Giulio and I did with the water on the floor. I wondered if this kind of action painting enabled us to find an early piece of his frozen pain buried at full fathom five underneath his scribbles. Giulio wanted to repeat our water painting several times. He gradually introduced some variations and not only allowed me to participate but also actively looked for my cooperation. When he went back to scribbling on a piece of paper, the transformation that stood out in his scribble drawings struck me deeply (see Figure 8.1). In the whirlpool of round marks, through which movement gave shape to what we could not yet call his pain, small circles started to

Figure 8.1 Squiggle with objects

appear. I viewed them as included and scattered fragments of emotional objects that could be perceived in a jumble of confused sensations.

Projecting and introjecting: how to create space-time

To share with Giulio what was going on – that is, the transformations of forms of proto-containment into forms of psychic containment – I decided to hang his drawings on the wall so that they would appear in their sequence and we might seize even the slightest transformation in the repetition.

Repetition in art is the way by which the artist explores reality and tries to study the light, the composition or the slightest formal transformations through the reiteration of a subject. In sequencing Giulio's drawings, I was looking for a form of time dimension and, at the same time, I hung together scribbles with similar details, creating a wide area of overlapping drawings on the wall.[19] The exasperating repetition looked to me not only like a defensive attempt but also like Giulio's desperate cry to follow him into an area of the mind where the thing-in-itself undergoes the first process of falsification, where a function collects some elements of the real world and lets others go, where dream initiates the first aesthetic processing of sensation. On the wall, I was doing something similar to one of the fundamental operations that allow for symbolization: to extract what is the same from what is different. A few weeks later, Giulio started to hang his drawings by himself, arranging them in a different relationship from the one I had introduced. Giulio was creating something defensive on the wall through spatial confusion of accidentally overlapping scribbles, and he looked for some relationship between them. When I had arranged his drawings, I was looking for a relationship between figurative traces. Now I realized that Giulio was looking for a relationship between the shape of the sheets or the shape of the small circles or rectangles represented in the scribbles according to his own sensitivity. Tustin described this specific trait of autistic children well when she observed how they reconstruct a jigsaw by the indentation of the pieces rather than by looking for a coherent subject matter.[20]

A performance by Marcel Duchamp in 1942, titled *Mile of String*, inspired me, and I started to connect the drawings with string in an attempt to relate his linking patterns with mine. In the meanwhile, I explained to Giulio what I was doing in very simple words. In 1942, Duchamp's performance[21] turned into a thick tangle of strings linking the art pieces on view in the first surrealist exhibition. On the opening day, the public was faced with a thick web of string that prevented them from seeing the works of art. This distancing was intentionally emphasized by the artist through the presence of children jumping rope.

What I wanted to do with Giulio was to open up the possibility of a concrete experience where the drawings, the movement and the obstacle that prevented sharing a symbolic element were all represented together. The form on which Giulio and I continued to work, along with other experiences, described in my view a shared pre-symbolic psychic space full of obstacles and mutual attempts to find one another. Repetition was not only a defence now but also a connecting string that enabled us to find the necessary trust to create a relationship between different ways of working through the experience and surrendering to each other. The transformation of a domination-submission dynamic into an interaction inhabited by dawning trust was what I was most aware of. This process lasted a few months and finally enabled Giulio to make his first real drawing (see Figure 8.2).

It was a very simple drawing and yet it attested, in my view, to the birth of space. Giulio had been able to draw things derived from the language of the sensory experience of rhythmicity, but at the same time, he had produced an experience where a new image had emerged. This image had no link to the drawings he had previously made. Bion names this

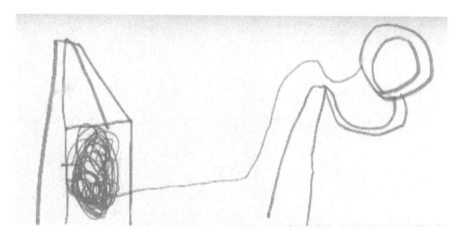

Figure 8.2 Pole voltage and electric wire

process "*evolution*".²² It indicates the birth of memory understood as the functional structure capable of fixing emotions. To fix emotions through a sensory image corresponds to the dawning ability to dream – that is, the ability to use α function and ♀/♂. Therefore, dreaming can produce changes in the functional structures of memory and promote the growth of the formal qualities in the symbolization process.²³ In a relatively short time, Giulio was able to strengthen his ability to negotiate space and to use the piece of paper to produce reasonable and recognizable representations. This graphic evolution went with the possibility of interacting with me through language, at least now and then. In addition to the use of space, he was increasingly more aware of time and the consequentiality of actions. This achievement had a remarkable nourishing effect in relational terms, and Giulio showed it on several occasions. The creation of an image in his mind was now expressed in his enthusiasm for things such as television and video cameras. He thus associated their representation with his old on-and-off experience that had engaged him for years and had provided him with the very first form-giving process of his psychic functioning. His capacity to be nourished and to look for nourishment through contact – that allowed a processing of experience through a real function of containment – found an expressive form in his drawings (see Figure 8.3).

Figure 8.3 Orange juice extractor

The meter

In the fourth year of analysis, Giulio was able to draw and play in a fuller and more differentiated way. He could depict his house from within and without, as if he were more aware of inside/outside, showing greater ability to deal with being separated. His old need for repetition was still visible in the graphic reiteration of an element that Giulio experienced as a core factor he could not give up: the electricity meter. This element, in his words, performed a function of regulating electricity, contacting and transforming electrical impulses with different destinations. He drew the meter first, as if it were a prerequisite to deal with him relating to the piece of paper and the various objects that he would then depict. The meter always carried the idea of connection, and sometimes, it also expressed his old need to adhere (see Figure 8.4).

When Giulio was drawing, I often fantasized that this object could be a figurative derivative of the progressive and slow maturation of his containment function. I wondered how I could facilitate the transformation of the necessary sensory support, favouring its functioning as an activator of the containment function.

As I went over my notes from those years, I thought about the first time when Giulio had dealt with anxiety-ridden emptiness and had given up the safe containment of the glass in order to find a wider and more uncertain support directly on the floor. I began to propose something similar when he was drawing, imagining that the piece of paper now embodied something

Action across emptiness 143

Figure 8.4 The connected meter

similar, though on a different level, to what the glass had represented for him. Giulio loved the constant shape of the sheet, its being blank and spotless. He expressed the same love for perfection in his drawings that were always very thorough.

I started to put another piece of paper near his sheet, placed at an angle against a book, or a piece of paper that was first crumpled up and then smoothed out. Sometimes I drew by his side and told him how being together can occur in a variety of ways: adhering to each other or being close with our bodies, being mirrored, being understood. I also prompted him to consider the empty space separating his drawing and mine. I would tell him how sometimes his orders made me feel withdrawn inside, about the fear of not finding each other and the trust whereby we had learned to recognize each other. At first, Giulio ignored my comments, but later, he started to take them in, and he developed a sounder trust in dealing with what was new. A drawing Giulio made in the spring during his seventh year of analysis was the most touching evidence of how he was less frightened about emptiness and how he could reach out beyond his own boundaries (see Figure 8.5).

In addition to the graphic evolution through which I tried to show the development of his ability for psychic containment, at the end of his

Figure 8.5 Meter with free-floating strings

treatment, Giulio was able to relate and sometimes to play with his peers and to attend school, as he was following an individualized syllabus. The relationship with his mother had also changed profoundly, and they were able to enjoy time together without considering their relationship exclusive. An important role in Giulio's progress was the fact that his mother had been able to confront and overcome the grief that had struck her.

Performing the shell

We can imagine that the forms of sensory self-containment that Tustin observed in autistic children and described as *"shells"* – sensory forms without psychic implication – can express the functioning of the proto-container. The therapist needs to make sense of these forms so as not to be overwhelmed by the feeling of despairing repetitiveness that these forms generate. However, verbal expression and symbolic form, which are the natural product of psychic transformation in the analyst's mind, cannot engage the functioning of the patient. The possibility of taking effective action in this direction goes through the therapist's experience of letting his own body be overwhelmed and transformed through an act of faith into a feeling of trustful surrendering. The therapeutic action ensuring these processes is close to an art performance, a form of art through the body where the artist does not know the final outcome of his artwork. He needs to open up to the possibility to surrender in the presence of the other, integrating the latter in his own mind and actions without being overwhelmed. An art performance does not aim to bridge the gap between oneself and the audience with an object loaded with meaning. It rather opens up the possibility of keeping a gap where the audience put in place, together with the artist, a creative action that goes through him. In the child, actions similar to art performances can facilitate the link between proto-container and container and can promote the functioning of the projective and introjective mechanism, which, in turn, activates and enhances a function. To me, Giulio's drawings seemed extraordinary evidence of this birth.

Notes

1 Nik Wallenda, *Balance: A Story of Faith, Family and Life on the Line*, New York: Hachette, 2013.
2 Tustin 1986.
3 Bion 1963, p. 23.
4 Bion 1989, p. 7.
5 Bion 1963, Cartwright 2010.
6 Bion 1962a, 1992.
7 Winnicott 1958d, p. 302.
8 Mitrani 2006.
9 Cohen and Jay 1996, Mastella 2012, Van Buren 1997.
10 Ghent 1990, p. 108.
11 Bion 1970, p. 35; Neri 2005.
12 Tustin 1994a.
13 Tustin 1994b, p. 121.
14 Mitrani 2006.
15 Grotstein 1983, Maiello 2001, Tustin 1981.
16 Alvarez 1992, 1999; Mitrani 1998.
17 Devoto Oli 1971.
18 Hamilton 1992.
19 On the wall of my office, I did something similar to what David Hookney did in his studio when he wanted to find a visual confirmation of his hypothesis as an art critic about the use of optical instruments in making paintings that became popular in the fourteenth century (see Hockney 2001).
20 Mitrani 2006, Tustin 1984, p. 281.
21 See http://blogfigures.blogspot.it/2010/11/mile-of-string.html (accessed January 28, 2016).
22 Bion 1992, p. 291.
23 Rocha Barros 2000.

Bibliography

Altman, N. Relational horizons in child psychoanalysis. *Journal of Infant, Child & Adolescent Psychotherapy*, 2:29–38, 2002.

Alvarez, A. *Live Company: Psychoanalytic Psychotherapy with Autistic, Borderline, Deprived and Abused Children*. Routledge, London, 1992.

Alvarez, A. Frustrations and separateness, delight and connectedness: Reflections on the conditions under which bad and good surprises are conductive to learning. *Journal of Child Psychotherapy*, 25(2):183–198, 1999.

Alvarez, A. *The Thinking Heart: Three Levels of Psychoanalytic Therapy with Disturbed Children*. Routledge, London, 2012.

Ambrosiano, L. L'intreccio tra teoria ed esperienza clinica [The intersection of theory and clinical experience]. *Rivista di Psicoanalisi*, 44:41–66, 1998.

Amir, D. From mother tongue to language. *Psychoanalytic Review*, 97:657–678, 2010.

Anzieu, D. *Le moi-peau*. Dunod, Paris, 1985.

Anzieu-Premmereur, C. Peter, the child who could not dream. *Psychoanalytic Inquiry*, 36:231–238, 2016.

Badoni, M. Parents and their child and the analyst in the middle: Working with a transgenerational mandate. *International Journal of Psycho-Analysis*, 83:1111–1131, 2002.

Baraldi, A.M.F., F. Manifredini, and L. Zagagnoni, eds. *Vanessa Bell & Virginia Woolf: disegnare la vita*. Comune di Ferrara, Civiche gallerie d'arte moderna e contemporanea, Ferrara, 1996.

Baranger, M. and W. Baranger. La situation analitica como campo dinamico [Analytic situation as dynamic field]. *Revista Uruguaya de Psicoanálisis*, 4(1):3–54, 1961–62.

Beebe, B. My journey in infant research and psychoanalysis: Microanalysis, a social microscope. *Psychoanalytic Psychology*, 31:4–25, 2014.

Beebe, B. and F. Lachmann. Organizing principles of interaction from infant research and the lifespan prediction of attachment: Application to adult treatment. *Journal of Infant, Child & Adolescent Psychotherapy*, 2:61–89, 2002.

Beebe, B. and F. Lachmann. The relational turn in psychoanalysis: A dyadic systems view from infant research. *Contemporary Psychoanalysis*, 39:379–409, 2003.

Benni, S. *La compagnia dei celestini*. Feltrinelli, Milano, 1992.
Bezoari, M. and A. Ferro. Mots, images, affects: L'aventure du sens dans la rencontre analytique. *Canadian Journal of Psychoanalysis*, 4(1):49–73, 1996.
Billow, R. M. A falsifying adolescent. *Psychoanalytic Quarterly*, 73:1041–1078, 2004.
Bion, W. R. *Experiences in Groups and Other Papers*. Tavistock, London, 1961.
Bion, W. R. The psycho-analytic study of thinking. *International Journal of Psycho-Analysis*, 43:306–310, 1962a.
Bion, W. R. *Learning from Experience*. Tavistock, London, 1962b.
Bion, W. R. *Elements of Psychoanalysis*. Heinemann, London, 1963.
Bion, W. R. *Transformations: Change from Learning to Growth*. Heinemann, London, 1965.
Bion, W. R. *Second Thoughts: Selected Papers on Psychoanalysis*. Heinemann, London, 1967.
Bion, W. R. *Attention and Interpretation: A Scientific Approach to Insight in Psycho-Analysis and Groups*. Tavistock, London, 1970.
Bion, W. R. *The Long Week-End 1897–1919: Part of a Life*. Fleetwood, Abingdon, 1982.
Bion, W. R. *Two Papers: The Grid and Caesura*. Karnac, London, 1989.
Bion, W. R. *Cogitations*. Karnac, London, 1992.
Bleger, J. *Simbiosis y ambiguedad, estudio psicoanalitico [Symbiosis and Ambiguity, a Psychoanalytic Study]*. Paidos, Buenos Aires, 1967.
Bloom, K. Movement as a medium for psychophysical integration. *Free Associations*, 8B:151–169, 2000.
Blum, H. P. Little Hans: A centennial review and reconsideration. *Journal of the American Psychoanalytical Association*, 55:749–765, 2007.
Bollas, C. *The Shadow of the Object: Psychoanalysis of the Unthought Known*. Columbia UP, New York, 1987.
Bonaminio, V., T. Carratelli, and A. Giannotti. *Fantasie dei genitori e psicopatologia dei figli*, chapter Equilibrio e rottura dell'equilibrio nella relazione tra fantasie inconsce dei genitori e sviluppo normale e patologico del bambino, pages 67–89. Borla, Roma, 1989.
Bonoviz, C. The cocreation of phantasy and the trasformation of psychic structure. *Psychoanalytic Dialogues*, 14:553–580, 2004.
Bourgeois, L. *Maman*. Wanas Foundation and Atlantis, Stockolm, 2007.
Brady, M. T. The individual in the group: An application of Bion's group theory to parent work in child analysis and child psychotherapy. *Contemporary Psychoanalysis*, 47:420–437, 2011.
Brown, L. J. Ruptures in the analytic setting and disturbances in the transformational field of dreams. *Psychoanalytic Quarterly*, 84:841–865, 2015.
Cartwright, D. *Containing States of Mind: Exploring Bion's Container Model in Psychoanalytic Psychotherapy*. Routledge, London and New York, 2010.
Charles, M. Auto-sensuous shapes: Prototypes for creative forms. *American Journal of Psychoanalysis*, 61:239–269, 2001.

Chazan, S. E. Searching for togetherness: The simultaneous treatment of a mother and her early adolescent daughter. *Psychoanalytic Inquiry*, 26:70–91, 2006.

Civitarese, G. Immersion versus interactivity and analytic field. *International Journal of Psycho-Analysis*, 89:279–298, 2008.

Civitarese, G. *The Intimate Room: Theory and Technique of the Analytic Field.* Routledge, London, 2010.

Civitarese, G. *Losing Your Head: Abjection, Aesthetic Conflict, and Psychoanalytic Criticism.* Rowman & Littlefield, Lanham, MD, 2014.

Civitarese, G. Transformations in hallucinosis and the receptivity of the analyst. *International Journal of Psycho-Analysis*, 96:1091–1116, 2015.

Cohen, D. and S. M. Jay. Autistic barriers in the psychoanalysis of borderline adults. *International Journal of Psycho-Analysis*, 77:913–933, 1996.

Corrao, F. *Introduction to Experiences in Groups.* Armando, Roma, 1971.

Corrao, F. Morphology and transformations of psychoanalytic models. *Rivista di Psicoanalisi*, 35:512–544, 1989.

Corrao, F. *Modelli psicoanalitici: mito, passione, memoria.* Laterza, Roma-Bari, 1992.

Corrao, F. *Orme*, volume II, chapter Duale-gruppale, pages 166–183. Cortina, Milano, 1998.

Davies, J. M. Erotic overstimulation and the co-construction of sexual meanings in transference-countertransference experience. *Psychoanalytic Quarterly*, 70:757–788, 2001.

Davies, N. and G. Eagle. Conceptualizing the paternal function: Maleness, masculinity, or thirdness? *Contemporary Psychoanalysis*, 49:559–585, 2013.

Decobert, S. and F. Sacco. *Dessin dans le travail psychanalytique avec l'enfant.* Eres, Ramonville Saint-Agne, 1995.

Devoto Oli. *Vocabolario della Lingua Italiana [Dictionary of Italian Language].* Torino: Le Monnier, 1971.

Di Ceglie, G. R. Orientation, containment and the emergence of symbolic thinking. *International Journal of Psycho-Analysis*, 94:1077–1091, 2013.

Di Renzo, M. and I. E. Nastasi. *Il movimento disegna.* Armando, Roma, 1989.

Diamond, M. J. Boys to men: The maturing of masculine gender identity through paternal watchful protectiveness. *Gender and Psychoanalysis*, 2:443–468, 1997.

Edelman, B. *L'adieu aux arts: rapport sur l'affaire Brâncuşi.* L'Herne, Paris, 2001.

Fabozzi, P. In-between: Shapes of subjectivities in the analytic situation. *Psychoanalytic Inquiry*, 35:578–596, 2015.

Fairbairn, W. R. D. *Psychoanalytic Studies of the Personality.* Tavistock, London, 1952.

Ferro, A. Il dialogo analitico: costituzione e trasformazione di mondi possibili. *Rivista di Psicoanalisi*, 40:389–409, 1994.

Ferro, A. *Seeds of Illness and Seeds of Recovery.* Brunner Routledge, London, 2004.

Ferro, A. Which reality in the psychoanalytic session? *Psychoanalytic Quarterly*, 74:421–442, 2005.

Ferro, A. Clinical implication in Bion's thought. *International Journal of Psycho-Analysis*, 87:989–1003, 2006.

Ferro, A. Book review: A beam of intense darkness by James S. Grotstein. *International Journal of Psycho-Analysis*, 89:867–888, 2008a.

Ferro, A. The patient as the analyst's best colleague: Transformation into a dream and narrative transformations. *The Italian Psychoanalytic Annual*, 2:199–205, 2008b.

Ferro, A. and R. Basile. Unity of analysis: Similarities and differences in the analysis of children and grown-ups. *Psychoanalytic Quarterly*, 75:477–500, 2006.

Ferro, A. and G. Foresti. Objects and characters in psychoanalytical text/dialogues. *International Forum of Psychoanalysis*, 17:71–81, 2008.

Feyerabend, P. K. *Three Dialogues on Knowledge*. Blackwell, Oxford, 1991.

Fonagy, P. and M. Target. Playing with reality: I. Theory of mind and the normal development of psychic reality. *International Journal of Psycho-Analysis*, 77:217–233, 1996.

Forrester, J. *Truth Games: Lies, Money and Psychoanalysis*. Harvard UP, Cambridge, MA, 1997.

Frankel, J. B. The play's the thing: How the essential processes of therapy are seen most clearly in child therapy. *Psychoanalytic Dialogues*, 8:149–182, 1998.

Freud, S. Analysis of a phobia in a five year-old boy. *Standard Edition*, 10:5–149, 1909.

Freud, S. On the history of the psycho-analytic movement. *Standard Edition*, 14:7–66, 1914.

Freud, S. The resistances to psycho-analysis. *Standard Edition*, 19:211–224, 1925.

Freud, S. An outline of psycho-analysis. *Standard Edition*, 23:139–208, 1938.

Gaddini, E. Early defensive fantasies and the psychoanalytical process. *International Journal of Psycho-Analysis*, 63:379–388, 1982.

Gaines, R. *Handbook of Interpersonal Psychoanalysis*, chapter The treatment of children, pages 751–770. Analytic Press, New York, 1995.

Galatzer-Levy, R. M. The nuts and bolts of child psychoanalysis. *Annual of Psychoanalysis*, 36:189–202, 2008.

Ghent, E. Masochism, submission, surrender: Masochism as a perversion of surrender. *Contemporary Psycho Analysis*, 26:108–136, 1990.

Godbout, C. Reflections on Bion's elements of psychoanalysis: Experience, thought and growth. *International Journal of Psycho-Analysis*, 85:1123–1136, 2004.

Golberg, P. Successful, dissociation, pseudovitality, and inauthentic use of the senses. *Psychoanalytic Dialogues*, 5:493–510, 1995.

Greenberg, J. Psychoanalytic interaction. *International Journal of Psycho-Analysis*, 16:25–38, 1996.

Greenberg, J. Is the transference feared by the psychoanalyst? *International Journal of Psycho-Analysis*, 78:1–14, 1997.

Greenberg, J. Commentary on Jose Bleger's theory and practice in psychoanalysis: Psychoanalytic praxis. *International Journal of Psycho-Analysis*, 93:1005–1016, 2012.

Grotstein, J. S. A proposed revision of the psychoanalytic concept of primitive mental states, part II: The borderline syndrome. Section 1: The disorders of autistic safety and symbiotic relatedness. *Contemporary Psychoanalysis*, 19:580–604, 1983.

Grotstein, J. S. The light militia of the lower sky. *Psychoanalytic Dialogues*, 14:99–118, 2004a.

Grotstein, J. S. The seventh servant: The implications of a truth drive in Bion's theory of 'O'. *International Journal of Psycho-Analysis*, 85:1081–1101, 2004b.

Grotstein, J. S. Projective transidentification. *International Journal of Psycho-Analysis*, 86:1051–1069, 2005.

Grotstein, J. S. *A Beam of Intense Darkness*. Karnac, London, 2007.

Grotstein, J. S. *Clinical Applications in the Kleinian/Bionian Mode*, volume 2, chapter But at the same time and on another level. Karnac, London, 2009.

Guignard, F. *Au vif de l'infantile*. Delachaux & Niestle, Lausanne, 1997.

Guntrip, H. *Schizoid Phenomena, Object-Relations and the Self*. International UP, Madison, CT, 1968.

Halpert, E. On lying and the lie of a toddler. *Psychoanalytic Quarterly*, 68:659–675, 2000.

Hamilton, V. The protective shell in children and adults: By Frances Tustin. *International Journal of Psycho-Analysis*, 73:173–176, 1992.

Hanly, C. The concept of truth in psychoanalysis. *International Journal of Psycho-Analysis*, 71:375–383, 1990.

Hellman, I., R. Grinberg, M. James, A. Maenchen, A. J. Solnit, and E. Kesternberg. Panel: The role of aggression in child analysis. *International Journal of Psycho-Analysis*, 53:321–323, 1972.

Hobson, R. P. and J. A. Meyer. Foundations for self and other: A study in autism. *Developmental Science*, 8:481–491, 2005.

Hockney, D. *Secret Knowledge: Rediscovering the Lost Techniques of the Old Masters*. Thames & Hudson, New York, 2001.

Holder, A. Preoedipal contributions to the formation of the superego. *Psychoanalytic Study of the Child*, 37:245–272, 1982.

Hopkins, L. B. Masud Khan's application of Winnicott's play techniques to analytic consultation and treatment of adults. *Contemporary Psychoanalysis*, 36:639–663, 2000.

Joseph, B. *Psychic Equilibrium and Psychic Change: Selected Papers of Betty Joseph*. Tavistock Routledge, London and New York, 1989.

Joseph, B. Thinking about a playroom. *Journal of Child Psychotherapy*, 24:359–366, 1998.

Kaës, R. La realité psychique du lien. *Le Divan familial*, 22:109–125, 2009.

Klein, M. *The Psycho-Analysis of Children*. Hogarth, London, 1932.

Knight, R. Margo and me II: The role of narrative building in child analytic technique. *Psychoanalytic Study of the Child*, 58:133–164, 2003.

Krimendahl, E. K. Metaphor in child psychoanalysis: Not simply a means to an end. *Contemporary Psychoanalysis*, 34:49–66, 1998.

Kuhn, T. S. *The Structure of Scientific Revolutions*. University of Chicago Press, Chicago and London, 1962.

Lachmann, F. and B. Beebe. Three principles of salience in the patient-analyst interaction. *Psychoanalytic Psychology*, 13:1–22, 1996.

Laplanche, J. *Life and Death in Psychoanalysis*. Johns Hopkins UP, Baltimore, MD, and London, 1976.

Lemma, A. The many faces of lying. *International Journal of Psycho-Analysis*, 86:737–753, 2005.

Lyons-Ruth, K. The two-person unconscious: Intersubjective dialogue, enactive relational representation, and the emergence of new forms of relational organization. *Psychoanalytic Inquiry*, 19:576–617, 1999.

McEwan, I. *The Daydreamer*. Anchor Book, New York, 1994.

Mahon, E. A good hour in child analysis and adult analysis. *Psychoanalytic Study of the Child*, 55:124–142, 2000.

Maiello, S. Prenatal trauma and autism. *Journal of Child Psychotherapy*, 27:107–124, 2001.

Mastella, M. Il bambino che venue dal freddo e che attraversò il vuoto [The child who came from the cold and across the emptiness]. *Rivista di Psicoanalisi*, 58:1017–1044, 2012.

Meltzer, D. *The Psychoanalytical Process*. [s.n.], London, 1967.

Milner, M. *On Not Being Able to Paint*. International UP, Madison, CT, 1950.

Mitrani, J. L. Never before and never again: The compulsion to repeat, the fear of breakdown and the defensive organization. *International Journal of Psycho-Analysis*, 79:301–316, 1998.

Mitrani, J. L. *Some Implication of the Work of Francis Tustin for the Psychoanalytic Treatment of Adult Patients*. 3rd Conference Frances Tustin Memorial Trust, Venice, 2006.

Miura, K. Folds – the basis of origami. *Symmetry: Culture and Science*, 5(1):13–22, 1994.

Modell, A. H. The holding environment and the therapeutic action of psychoanalysis. *Journal of the American Psychoanalytic Association*, 24:285–307, 1976.

Modell, A. H. The psychoanalytic setting as a container of multiple levels of reality: A perspective on the theory of psychoanalytic treatment. *Psychoanalytic Inquiry*, 9:67–87, 1989.

Molinari, E. The use of child drawings to explore the dual group analytic field in child analysis. *International Journal of Psycho-Analysis*, 94:293–312, 2013a.

Molinari, E. *Psicoanalisi oggi: Teoria e tecnica*, chapter Variazioni sul tema: l'analisi infantile e dell'adolescente, chapter in Ferro, A. et al., Psicoanalisi oggi. Teoria e tecnica, pages 261–307. Carocci Editore, Rome, 2013b.

Neri, C. Libere associazioni, catene associative e pensiero di gruppo [Free associations, associative chains and group thought]. *Rivista di Psicoanalisi*, 48:387–402, 2002.

Neri, C. What is the function of faith and trust in psychoanalysis? *International Journal of Psycho-Analysis*, 86:79–97, 2005.

Neri, C. La nozione allargata di campo in psicoanalisi. *Rivista di Psicoanalisi*, 53:103–134, 2007.

Nicholsen, S. W. Working with stone, working with psyche: The role of reverie in the process of making art and working with patients. *Rivista di Psicoanalisi*, 61:209–223, 2015.

Nishiyama, Y. Miura folding: Applying origami to space exploration. *International Journal of Pure and Applied Mathematics*, 79:269–279, 2012.

Nissim Momigliano, L. N. Il setting: tema con variazioni [The setting: A theme with variations]. *Rivista di Psicoanalisi*, 34:605–683, 1988.

Nissim Momigliano, L. N. *Shared Experience: The Psychoanalytic Dialogue*, chapter Two people talking in a room: An investigation on the analytic dialogue, pages 5–20. Karnac, London, 1992.

Norman, J. The psychoanalyst and the baby: A new look at work with infants. *International Journal of Psycho-Analysis*, 82:83–100, 2001.

Novick, K. and J. Novick. *Working with Parents Makes Therapy Work*. Aronson, New York, 2005.

Ogden, T. H. The mother, the infant and the matrix: Interpretations of aspects of the work of Donald Winnicott. *Contemporary Psychoanalysis*, 21:346–371, 1985.

Ogden, T. H. Misrecognitions and the fear of not knowing. *Psychoanalytic Quarterly*, 57:643–666, 1988.

Ogden, T. H. On the concept of an autistic-contiguous position. *International Journal of Psycho-Analysis*, 70:127–140, 1989.

Ogden, T. H. *The Matrix of the Mind: Object Relations and the Psychoanalytic Dialogue*. Karnac, London, 1992.

Ogden, T. H. The analytic third: Working with intersubjective clinical facts. *International Journal of Psycho-Analysis*, 75:3–19, 1994.

Ogden, T. H. *Reverie and Interpretation: Sensing Something Human*. Jason Aronson, Northvale, NJ, 1997.

Ogden, T. H. Reading Winnicott. *Psychoanalytic Quarterly*, 70:299–323, 2001.

Ogden, T. H. What's true and whose idea was it. *International Journal of Psycho-Analysis*, 84:593–606, 2003.

Ogden, T. H. An introduction to the reading of Bion. *International Journal of Psycho-Analysis*, 85:285–300, 2004a.

Ogden, T. H. On holding and containing, being and dreaming. *International Journal of Psycho-Analysis*, 85:1349–1364, 2004b.

Ogden, T. H. The analytic third: Implication for psychoanalytic theory and technique. *Psychoanalytic Quarterly*, 73:167–195, 2004c.

Ogden, T. H. On talking-as-dreaming. *International Journal of Psycho-Analysis*, 88:575–589, 2007.

O'Shaughnessy, E. Can a liar be psychoanalysed? *International Journal of Psycho-Analysis*, 71:187–195, 1990.

Otte, M. J. The child psychoanalyst as clinician: The perils of parental projection. *Annual of Psychoanalysis*, 26:201–217, 1999.

Pellizzari, G. L'invenzione della verità tra infanzia e adolescenza. *Richard & Piggle*, 1:29–41, 2010.

Petrella, F. *Turbamenti affettivi e alterazioni dell'esperienza [Emotional Turmoil and the Distortion of Experience]*, chapter Quadro e cornice: il setting clinico [The picture and the frame: The clinical setting], pages 127–141. Cortina, Milano, 1993.

Phillips, A. *Winnicott*. Harvard UP, Cambridge, MA, 1988.

Racalbuto, A. *Tra il fare e il dire. L'esperienza dell'inconscio e del non verbale in psicoanalisi*. Cortina, Milano, 1994.

Riolo, F. Truth, lying and analytic thought. *Rivista di Psicoanalisi*, 27:727–738, 1981.

Rocha Barros, E. Affect and pictographic image: The constitution of meaning in mental life. *International Journal of Psycho-Analysis*, 81:1087–1099, 2000.

Salo, F. T. Recognizing the infant as subject in infant-parent psychotherapy. *International Journal of Psycho-Analysis*, 88:961–979, 2007.

Salomonsson, B. Talk to me baby, tell me what's the matter now. *International Journal of Psycho-Analysis*, 88:127–146, 2007.

Schacht, L. La capacità di sorprendersi [The capacity to be surprised]. *Richard & Piggle*, 9:2, 2000.

Sharpe Freeman, E. *Dream Analysis: A Practical Handbook for Psycho-Analysts*. Hogarth Press, Institute of Psycho-Analysis, London, 1978.

Slade, A. *Children and Play: Clinical and Developmental Approaches to Meaning and Representation*, chapter Making meaning and making believe: Their role in the clinical process, pages 81–110. Oxford UP, Oxford, 1994.

Spence, D. P. *Narrative Truth and Historical Truth: Meaning and Interpretation in Psychoanalysis*. Norton, New York, 1982.

Stensson, J. Aniara, mimicry and aspect-seeing. *International Forum of Psychoanalysis*, 15:157–161, 2006.

Stern, D. N. The goal and structure of mother-infant play. *Journal of the American Academy of Child Psychiatry*, 13:402–421, 1974.

Stern, D. N. *The First Relationship: Infant and Mother*. Open Books, London, 1977.

Stern, D. N. *The Interpersonal World of the Infant: A View from Psychoanalysis and Developmental Psychology*. Basic Books, New York, 1985.

Stern, D. N. Affect in the context of the infant's lived experience: Some considerations. *International Journal of Psycho-Analysis*, 69(2):233–238, 1988.

Stern, D. N., L. W. Sander, J. P. Nahum, A. M. Harrison, K. Lyons-Ruth, A. C. Morgan, N. Bruschweilerstern, and E. Z. Tronick. Non-interpretive mechanisms in psychoanalytic therapy: The 'something more' than interpretation. *International Journal of Psycho-Analysis*, 79:903–921, 1998.

Stokes, A. *New Directions in Psycho-Analysis*, chapter The form in art, pages 61–68. Tavistock, London, 1955.

Sugarman, A. Dimensions of the child analyst's role as a developmental object: Affect regulation and limit setting. *Psychoanalytic Study of the Child*, 58:189–213, 2003.

Tisseron, S. *Les contenants de pensee*, chapter Schemes d'enveloppe et schemes de transformation dans le fantasme et dans la cure, pages 35–54. Dunod, Paris, 1993.

Tisseron, S. All writing is drawing: The spatial development of the manuscript. *Yale French Studies*, 84:29–42, 1994.

Tomasi di Lampedusa, G. *I racconti*. Feltrinelli, Milano, 1961.

Tuch, R. H. Thinking with, and about, patients too scared to think: Can non-interpretive maneuvers stimulate reflective thought? *International Journal of Psycho-Analysis*, 88:91–111, 2007.

Tuch, R. H. Thinking outside the box: A metacognitive/theory of mind perspective on concrete thinking. *Journal of the American Psychoanalytic Association*, 59:765–789, 2011.

Tustin, F. *Autistic States in Children*. Routledge & Kegan Paul, London, and Boston, MA, 1981.

Tustin, F. Autistic shapes. *International Review of Psycho-Analysis*, 11:279–290, 1984.

Tustin, F. *Autistic Barriers in Neurotic Patients*. Karnac, London, 1986.

Tustin, F. The perpetuation of an error. *Journal of Child Psychotherapy*, 20:3–23, 1994a.

Tustin, F. Autistic children who are assessed as not brain-damaged. *Journal of Child Psychotherapy*, 20:103–131, 1994b.

Vallino, D. *Fare psicoanalisi con genitori e bambini [Consultation with the Child and His Parents]*. Borla, Roma, 2010.

Van Buren, J. *Encounters with Autistic States: A Memorial Tribute to Frances Tustin*, chapter Themes of being and not-being in the work of Frances Tustin and Jacques Lacan, pages 195–208. Jason Aronson, Northvale, NJ and London, 1997.

Wangh, M. International Journal of Psychoanalysis. XXIX, 1948: The nature and function of phantasy. Susan Isaacs. pp. 73–97. *Psychoanalytic Quarterly*, 19:19–606, 1950.

Weinshel, E. M. Some observations on not telling the truth. *Journal of the American Psychoanalytic Association*, 27:503–531, 1979.

Weiss, S. On the resistance to child analysis: Problems of the parent and the analyst. *Annual of Psychoanalysis*, 23:79–91, 1995.

Wilkinson, S. and G. Hough. Lie as narrative truth in abused adopted adolescents. *Psychoanalytic Study of the Child*, 51:580–596, 1996.

Winnicott, D. W. The observation of infants in a set situation. *International Journal of Psycho-Analysis*, 22:229–249, 1941.

Winnicott, D. W. Transitional objects and transitional phenomena: A study of the first not-me possession. *International Journal of Psycho-Analysis*, 34:89–97, 1953.

Winnicott, D. W. *Collected Papers: Through Paediatrics to Psycho-Analysis*, chapter Primitive emotional development [1945], pages 145–156. Hogarth, London, 1958a.

Winnicott, D. W. *Collected Papers: Through Paediatrics to Psycho-Analysis*, chapter Hate in the counter transference [1947], pages 194–203. Tavistock, London, 1958b.

Winnicott, D. W. *Collected Papers: Through Paediatrics to Psycho-Analysis*, chapter Metapsychological and clinical aspects of regression within the psycho-analytical set-up [1954], pages 278–294. Hogarth, London, 1958c.

Winnicott, D. W. *Collected Papers: Through Paediatrics to Psycho-Analysis*, chapter Primary maternal preoccupation [1956], pages 300–305. Tavistock, London, 1958d.

Winnicott, D. W. *The Maturational Processes and the Facilitating Environment: Studies in the Theory of Emotional Development*, chapter On the contribution of direct child observation to psycho-analysis [1957], pages 109–114. Hogarth, London, 1964a.

Winnicott, D. W. *The Maturational Processes and the Facilitating Environment: Studies in the Theory of Emotional Development*, chapter The capacity to be alone [1958], pages 29–36. Hogarth, London, 1964b.

Winnicott, D. W. *The Maturational Processes and the Facilitating Environment: Studies in the Theory of Emotional Development*, chapter Communicating and not communicating leading to a study of certain opposites [1963], pages 179–192. Hogarth Press, London, 1965a.

Winnicott, D. W. *The Maturational Processes and the Facilitating Environment: Studies in the Theory of Emotional Development*. Hogarth Press, London, 1965b.

Winnicott, D. W. *Playing and Reality*. Tavistock, London, 1971.

Winnicott, D. W. *Deprivation and Delinquency*, chapter The antisocial tendency [1956], pages 120–131. Routledge, London, 1984.

Winnicott, D. W. *Home Is Where We Start From*, chapter Living creatively, pages 35–54. New York: W. W. Norton Company, 1986.

Winnicott, D. W. *Psycho-Analytic Exploration*, chapter in Winnicott C., R. Shepherd, and M. Devis, The mother-infant experience of mutuality, pages 261–260. Harvard University Press, Cambridge, Massachusetts, 1989.

Woolf, V. *Monday or Tuesday*. Harcourt, Brace and Company, New York, 1921.

Woolf, V. *A Haunted House and Other Short Stories*. Hogarth, London, 1944.

Woolf, V. *Pictures in the Moment and Other Essays*. Hogarth, London, 1964.

Woolf, V. *A Change of Perspective: The Letters of Virginia Woolf 1923–1928*. Hogarth, London, 1994.

Index

action 4, 5, 7, 8, 11, 12, 51, 58, 68, 84, 112, 123, 124, 127, 128, 129, 134, 138, 144, 145
activity and passivity 3, 25, 29; *see also* transformation
adolescence 7, 61, 73
aesthetic 3, 5, 11, 14, 17, 32, 34, 50, 78, 89, 107, 109, 130, 139; *see also* art
affect 78, 153, 154; *see also* emotion
aggression 10, 43, 45, 90, 150
aggressive 27, 32, 42, 47, 117
aggressiveness 117, 122; *see also* violence
agoraphobia 16
aliveness 13, 27, 66, 117, 126, 135, 136
alpha element 3, 10, 12, 55, 59, 60–72, 76, 80, 92, 106, 131, 141
Altman, N. 109n27
Alvarez, A. 73n15, 128n2, 145n16
ambivalence 48, 52, 66, 90
Ambrosiano, L. 87n9, 109n10
Amir, D. 109n29
analytic field 2, 3, 4, 5, 6, 18, 19, 20, 23, 24, 25, 33, 36, 37, 38, 39, 42, 43, 46, 47, 50, 51, 52, 54, 55, 57, 58, 59, 60, 62, 63, 67, 68, 69, 72, 74, 75, 76, 77, 78, 80, 81, 82, 83, 85, 86, 88, 92, 93, 94, 98, 105, 106, 110, 114, 117, 124, 126, 127
Anderson, P. 54, 55, 60, 72n1
anxiety 10, 13, 28, 39, 44, 45, 65, 77, 78, 79, 91, 97, 104, 116, 117, 119, 120, 122, 123, 129, 130, 134, 135, 137; *see also* fear; fright; phobia
Anzieu, D. 22n20, 24, 34n2, 35n11
Anzieu-Premmereur, C. 22n20
art 1, 2, 9, 14, 20, 22, 31, 32, 37, 107, 134, 138, 139, 140, 144, 145; *see also* aesthetic
Atkinson, G. 109n21

autism 40, 63, 109, 130, 131, 132, 133, 134, 137, 140, 144
autistic-contiguous position 76
awareness 11, 12, 26, 37, 41, 42, 45, 61, 70, 83, 86, 88, 96, 101, 104, 106, 117, 125, 130, 140, 141, 142

Badoni, M. 109n2
Baharrier, H. 128n5
Baraldi, A. M. F. 22n7
Baranger, M. 52n2, 73n5, 109n26
Baranger, W. 52n2, 73n5, 109n26
Basile, R. 7, 22n18, 87n7
Beebe, B. 22n14, 53n15, 128n12
Bell, V. 2, 3, 4, 22n24
beta element 3, 16, 55, 59, 63, 67–72, 131, 132
Bezoari, M. 52n2
Billow, R. M. 73n23
binocular 102, 109
Bion, W. R. 3, 4, 22n8, n9, 37, 38, 51, 52n6, 53n25, 55, 56, 58, 59, 65, 67, 69, 73n6, n7, n20, n21, n30, n32, n35, n37, n38, 80, 87n13, n14, n15, 102, 109n16, n20, n22, n23, 127, 128n11, 131, 133, 140, 145n3, n4, n5, n6, n11, n22
birth 3, 12, 15, 16, 25, 29, 34, 50, 51, 56, 62, 79, 101, 111, 115, 116, 118, 131, 135, 140, 141, 145
Bleger, J. 87n6, 109n13
Bloom, K. 128n3
Blum, H. P. 22n4
body 6, 8, 9, 10, 11, 12, 13, 20, 21, 24, 25, 26, 27, 28, 29, 30, 32, 33, 34, 37, 41, 42, 45, 49, 50, 57, 61, 104, 111, 115, 123, 124, 126, 127, 130, 133, 134, 137, 144; and mind, relation between 41, 42, 50, 111, 123, 127, 130, 133, 134

Bollas, C. 26, 34n5
Bonaminio, V. 109n6
Bonoviz, C. 22n16
borderline 128n6
boundaries 8, 143
boundary 13, 21, 29, 31
Bourgeois, L. 116, 128n7
Brady, M. T. 109n1
Brâncusi, C. 14
breast 22, 34, 50, 83, 112, 130
Brown, L. J. 87n7
Bruschweilerstern, N. 22n14, 53n13

Calvin 110, 114, 116, 117, 118, 125, 128n1
camera 23, 74, 75, 76, 79, 81, 84, 85, 86, 87
Canaletto (Giovanni Antonio Canal *also known*) 86
Carratelli, T. 147
cartoon 110, 114, 118, 124, 125
Cartwright, D. 145n5
Charles, M. 35n10
Chazan, S. E. 109n3, 148
child 1, 2, 3, 4, 5, 6, 7, 8, 9, 10, 11, 12, 13, 14, 15, 16, 19, 20, 21, 22, 23, 24, 26, 30, 33, 34, 37, 38, 40, 41, 42, 48, 49, 50, 51, 52, 54, 55, 57, 61, 62, 64, 67, 68, 72, 79, 81, 82, 83, 84, 86, 88, 89, 90, 91, 92, 93, 94, 96, 98, 99, 101, 105, 106, 107, 111, 112, 113, 114, 115, 116, 117, 119, 120, 121, 122, 123, 124, 125, 126, 127, 129, 130, 132, 133, 135, 136, 137, 145; *see also* therapy, mother and child
childhood 12, 23, 29, 61, 62, 65, 66, 68, 93, 95
cinema 25, 121
Civitarese, G. 22n2, 87n5, 109n13
Cohen, D. 145n4
concreteness 18, 20, 21, 25, 27, 47, 48, 73, 76, 78, 79, 80, 109, 124, 130, 134, 140
conflict 2, 21, 57, 82, 148
conscious 5, 13, 38, 46, 50, 51, 52, 55, 57, 63, 65, 68, 74, 80, 81, 82, 85, 93, 101, 102, 109, 114, 117
consciousness 4, 30, 56, 64, 80, 86, 92
contact barrier 13, 38, 50, 51, 55, 76
container 6, 10, 26, 28, 31, 38, 49, 51, 52, 67, 69, 80, 109, 123, 132, 137, 145; development of 24, 25, 27, 80, 131, 133, 142, 143; *see also* proto-container
container-contained 38, 73
Corrao, F. 109n21, n25, n26, 128n14
countertransference 8, 26, 33, 91

creativity 6–9, 11, 21, 24, 25, 28, 33, 34, 35, 37, 38, 41, 42, 45, 47, 49, 50, 52, 62, 72, 79, 84, 93, 106, 107, 110, 112, 113, 118, 122, 123, 125, 126, 129, 134, 145; and transformation 25, 28, 62, 72, 89, 106, 107
curiosity 21, 74, 104, 122, 126, 127

Davies, J. M. 65, 73n24, n29
daydream 7, 18; *see also* phantasies
death 26, 32, 100, 105, 151
Decobert, S. 34n3
defence 9, 30, 39, 61, 63, 65, 77, 78, 80, 92, 94, 118, 123, 131, 140
depression 26, 135
depressive position 109
Derrida, J. 22n7
desire 4, 12, 13, 16, 19, 26, 31, 42, 48, 56, 57, 62, 63, 66, 68, 71, 123, 137
Devoto, G. 145n17
Diamond, M. J. 73n24
Di Ceglie, G. R. 128n13
digestive function 31, 34, 123
Di Renzo, M. 22n19
disintegration 115
dissociation 22, 126, 149
distortion 36, 57, 60, 62, 71
dream 3, 13, 14, 15, 19, 20, 22, 30, 38, 46, 51, 52, 55, 60, 61, 63, 67, 70, 76, 77, 92, 102, 107, 108, 114, 139, 141
Duchamp, M. 140

Eagle, G. 73n24
Edelman, B. 22n22, 148
ego 2, 24, 32, 56
emotion 5, 6, 8, 9, 10, 12, 14, 15, 16, 18, 19, 20, 31, 38, 39, 41, 42, 46, 47, 49, 51, 56, 64, 65, 67, 68, 70, 72, 77, 78, 89, 91, 92, 93, 94, 96, 99, 100, 101, 102, 106, 107, 109, 114, 116, 117, 118, 120, 122, 123, 124, 126, 127, 128, 130, 131, 134, 137, 141; *see also* affect
empathy 74
enactment 28, 46
evidence 25, 143, 145
expectation 24, 64, 118, 124, 131
experience 1, 4, 10, 11, 12, 14, 24, 25, 26, 27, 32, 34, 39, 41, 43, 44, 46, 48, 49, 50, 51, 52, 63, 65, 70, 74, 76, 77, 79, 80, 81, 85, 90, 92, 99, 104, 105, 107, 109, 110, 111, 113, 114, 115, 116, 119, 123, 124, 126, 127, 130, 131, 132, 133, 134, 137, 140, 141, 144

Fabozzi, P. 109n7
Fairbairn, W. R. D. 109n14
faith 61, 64, 129, 135, 144, 145
family 16, 17, 61, 62, 83, 86, 88, 89, 94, 97, 102, 103, 105, 109, 124, 126, 127, 129, 145
fantasies: body or primitive 28, 32, 42, 44, 50, 91, 96, 113, 127, 131
fantasy 9, 14, 24, 29, 30, 42, 44, 50, 56, 57, 62, 74, 80, 92, 94, 96, 103, 106, 131, 137
father 12, 13, 31, 56, 61, 62, 63, 81, 82, 83, 84, 86, 89, 90, 93, 95, 96, 98, 99, 103, 104, 106, 119, 128, 135
fear 9, 16, 18, 26, 30, 33, 48, 80, 87, 101, 116, 143; *see also* anxiety
feeling 8, 10, 13, 15, 16, 26, 27, 29, 30, 32, 37–44, 46, 47, 49, 50, 51, 52, 55, 61, 65, 67, 68, 71, 74, 78, 89, 90, 92, 93, 96, 97, 98, 99, 102, 104, 110, 112, 113, 115, 116, 117, 130, 132, 133, 134, 144
Ferro, A. 7, 22n15, n18, 38, 52n2, 53n9, n10, n15, 55, 59, 70, 73n4, n18, n39, 87n7, 92, 109n12, n26
Feyerabend, P. 53n23
Fonagy, P. 73n13
Foresti, G. 53n10
Forrester 73n14
Frankel, J. B. 22n13, 109n28
free-association 100, 101, 104, 126
Freud, S. 2, 3, 22n4, 56, 57, 73n10, n12, n31
fright 10, 18, 71, 82, 143; *see also* anxiety
function 2, 3, 6, 7, 10, 12, 26, 29, 31, 32, 33, 38, 47, 49, 55, 57, 67, 68, 73, 75, 76, 79, 80, 81, 86, 92, 106, 117, 131, 132, 133, 139, 141, 142, 145

Gaddini, E. 50, 53n20
Gaines, R. 22n13
Galatzer-Levy, R. M. 109n1
gender 44, 54, 61, 62, 71, 73
Ghent, E. 145n10
Giannotti, A. 109n6
Godbout, C. 73n34
Goisis 73n17
Golberg, P. 109n15
Gran Sasso National Laboratories 54
grasping 25, 65, 68, 71, 74, 86
Greenberg, J. 53n15, 87n6, 109n7
Grinberg, R. 150
Grotstein, J. S. 55, 59, 72n3, 73n5, n33, 87n7, 109n26, 128n11, 145n15
group 54, 82, 83, 86, 87, 88, 89, 90, 91, 93, 94, 96, 98, 99, 100, 101, 102, 103, 105, 106, 107, 115, 121, 124, 127; *see also* therapy, group
Guignard, F. 73n27
Guntrip, H. 109n15

hallucination 13, 130, 135
hallucinosis 109
Halpert, E. 73n13
Hamilton, V. 145n18
Hanly, C. 73n18
Harrison, A. M. 22n14, 53n13
hate 16, 18, 47, 61, 62, 66, 86, 87, 90–4, 96, 99, 104, 105, 109
Hellman, I. 109n24
Hiller 107, 108
Hobbes 110, 114, 116, 117, 118, 125, 128n1
Hobson, R. P. 35n9
Hockney, D. 87n4, 145n19
Hoffman, D. 63
Holder, A. 73n28
holding 9, 18, 75, 76, 79, 94, 100, 111, 115
Hopkins, L. B. 109n28
Hough, G. 73n17
house 10, 13, 21, 23, 32, 49, 81, 95, 116, 120, 142; *see also* container

identification 25, 26, 31, 58, 67, 75, 81, 92, 93, 131, 133, 134
illness 45, 81, 91, 132, 134
image 2, 4, 10, 12, 14, 15, 16, 17, 18, 20, 22, 23, 27, 28, 30, 33, 34, 36, 41, 42, 66, 75, 77, 78, 81, 85, 86, 92, 106, 107, 113, 116, 117, 118, 119, 122, 123, 124, 136, 140, 141
imitation 40, 41, 42, 50, 57, 136, 137
impotence 9, 39, 41, 43
integration 12, 134, 145
internal 5, 17, 27, 31, 49, 57, 58, 62, 67, 85, 92, 101, 112, 122, 124, 126
interpretation 6, 9, 10, 26, 27, 29, 51, 68, 94, 98, 102
intersubjective 38, 50, 51, 72, 76, 100, 102, 124, 127
intrapsychic 100, 130
intrasubjective 38, 51, 59
introjection 24, 132, 133, 139, 145
Isaacs 154

James, M. 109n24
Jay, S. M. 145n9
Joseph, B. 22n10

K *see* knowing
Kaës, R. 101, 102, 109n19
Klein, M. 2, 3, 22n5
Knight, R. 22n14
knowing 107, 127; *see also* transformation
Koryo 36
Krimendahl, E. K. 22n13
Kuhn, T. S. 53n23

L *see* loving
Lacan, J. 154
Lachmann, F. 22n14, 53n15, 128n12
Lampedusa 23, 34n1
Laplanche, J. 73n25
learning 10, 93, 94, 101, 110, 121, 132, 135, 137
Lemma, A. 57, 73n16
lie 45, 54–60, 62, 64, 65, 68, 70, 71, 72, 73, 79, 107, 112, 136, 138
loss 5, 12, 39, 40, 43, 47, 61, 68, 70, 78, 91, 99, 116, 126, 134, 135
love 1, 18, 30, 32, 51, 57, 64, 66, 71, 87, 92, 93, 96, 117, 143
loving 51, 100, 103
Lumière, L. 23, 26, 28, 34
Lyons-Ruth, K. 22n14, 53n13, 128n8

McEwan, I. 21, 22n25
McMeel 128n1
Maenchen, A. 109n24
Mahon, E. 22n2
Maiello, S. 145n15
Manifredini, F. 22n7
Mastella, M. 145n9
meanings 5, 6, 31, 33, 62, 87, 134
Meltzer, D. 87n8
memory 4, 12, 13, 26, 27, 30, 51, 55, 64, 65, 66, 68, 99, 101, 117, 141
mentalization 26
Meyer, J. A. 35n9
Milner, M. 6, 7, 8, 22n17, 29, 35n7, 87n11
mimicry 153
mind 4, 7, 10, 14, 16, 18, 20, 26, 29, 36, 37, 41, 54, 55, 56, 57, 59, 63, 64, 65, 66, 67, 70, 72, 74, 75, 76, 78, 79, 80, 93, 94, 104, 113, 117, 119, 125, 129, 130, 131, 133, 137, 138, 139, 141, 144, 145
Mitrani, J. L. 145n8, n14, n16, n20
Miura, K. 36, 37, 42, 52n3
Modell, A. H. 87n5
Molinari, E. 87n16, 128n9
Morgan, A. C. 22n14, 53n13
mother 6, 12, 13, 16, 18, 23, 24, 25, 26, 27, 28, 30, 32, 34, 38, 41, 42, 46, 48, 49, 50, 51, 61, 62, 63, 66, 67, 70, 71, 77, 79, 81, 82, 83, 84, 90, 93, 94, 95, 96, 98, 99, 101, 102, 103, 109, 111, 112, 113, 114, 115, 117, 122, 123, 125, 126, 129, 130, 131, 132, 133, 135, 136, 137, 144

Nahum, J. P. 22n14, 53n13
narcissistic 27
NASA 36
Nastasi, I. E. 22n19
Neri, C. 99, 109n18, 128n14, 145n11
neurosis 2, 24, 99, 154
Nicholsen, S. W. 22n2
nightmare 22, 64, 116
Nishiyama, Y. 52n3
Nissim Momigliano, L. N. 52n2, 87n9
Norman, J. 128n4
Novick, J. 109n1
Novick, K. 109n1
Nutella 89, 98, 104, 105, 109n5

O: transformation in 55, 58, 107, 124, 127, 150
object: external 18, 26, 29, 30, 32, 34, 38, 53, 58, 64, 66, 69, 71, 78, 87, 96, 117, 121, 131, 134, 136, 142; internal 57; subjective 41
Oedipus 3
Oedipus complex 56, 57, 71
Ogden, T. H. 19, 22n15, n23, 37, 38, 52n2, n4, 53n7, n8, n12, n15, n17, n23, 73n5, n8, n22, n36, 87n6, n8, 109n11, n13, 124, 128n10
Oli, G. 145n17
omnipotence 29, 30, 57, 58, 70
Ono, Y. 134
origami 36, 37, 151, 152
oscillation 15, 55, 67, 69, 105, 127, 129, 130, 131, 132, 133
O'Shaughnessy, E. 58, 73n19
Otte, M. J. 109n6

painting 1, 2, 7, 8, 14, 19, 20, 22, 82, 85, 138, 145
paranoid-schizoid 58, 65, 109
parents 16, 23, 24, 30, 31, 44, 47, 48, 49, 52, 61, 62, 71, 73, 78, 82, 83, 86, 88, 89, 90, 91, 92, 93, 95, 97, 98, 99, 100, 101, 103, 104, 105, 106, 107, 112, 124, 126
passivity and activity 16, 84
patient 1, 2, 11, 12, 14, 15, 17, 18, 19, 20, 22, 32, 38, 39, 41, 50, 52, 54, 56, 58, 65, 66, 74, 75, 76, 78, 80, 81, 85, 86, 87, 92,

99, 109, 110, 111, 112, 113, 115, 119, 126, 128, 130, 133, 134, 137, 144
Pellizzari, G. 73n11
Petrella, F. 49, 53n17
phantasies: unconscious 2, 3, 11
phantasy 2, 3, 6, 11, 14
Phillips, A. 53n18
phobia 56, 116, 149; *see also* anxiety
pictures 19, 23, 28, 33, 34, 118, 123
play 3, 4, 5, 6, 8, 9, 10, 18, 19, 20, 25, 29, 34, 36, 37, 38, 40, 41, 43, 44, 45, 46, 47, 48, 49, 50, 51, 52, 68, 70, 71, 80, 81, 82, 88, 89, 90, 93, 98, 106, 107, 110, 113, 114, 124, 132, 133, 142, 144
Pollock, J. 138
potential 24, 29, 41, 66, 111, 121, 131, 137
preconception 69, 131
projection 25, 61, 67, 75, 96, 131, 132, 133, 145
proto-container 69, 130–3, 139, 144, 145
psychotic 76, 109

Racalbuto, A. 34n4
reality 3, 4, 6, 16, 19, 30, 40, 57, 62, 65, 77, 80, 84, 86, 102, 103, 109, 113, 136, 139
reciprocity 21, 47, 50, 51
representation 5, 6, 10, 11, 12, 14, 20, 25, 27, 28, 30, 32, 75, 76, 83, 85, 100, 103, 107, 110, 123, 141
repression 2, 56
reverie 6, 7, 8, 20, 21, 51, 55, 60, 67, 68, 117
Richard 153
Riolo, F. 73n20
Robin Hood 104
Rocha Barros, E. 128n8, 145n23

Sacco, F. 34n3, 148
Salo, F. T. 128n8, 153
Salomonsson, B. 128n4
Sander, L. W. 22n14, 53n13
Schacht, L. 87n10
schizoid 96, 99, 150
self 10, 34, 38, 51, 57, 58, 64, 66, 71, 79, 96, 106, 113, 114, 137
setting 18, 19, 21, 42, 47, 49, 52, 55, 59, 72, 74, 75, 76, 77, 78, 79, 80, 81, 84, 85, 86, 87, 91, 99, 110, 112, 115, 119, 122, 124, 126, 127, 128, 135
sexuality 13, 31, 34, 56, 61, 62, 63, 71, 116
Shakespeare, W. 138
Sharpe Freeman, E. 35n9
skin 14, 34, 61

Slade, A. 22n13, 153
Solnit, A. J. 150
space 3, 5, 8, 16, 24, 27, 36, 38, 42, 45, 51, 55, 59, 60, 74, 75, 76, 77, 78, 79, 82, 85, 86, 101, 103, 110, 111, 112, 114, 117, 126, 129, 130, 131, 134, 137, 140, 141, 143; transitional 8, 38, 42, 48, 51, 75, 77
Spence, D. P. 73n18
splitting 65
Stensson, J. 53n21
Stern, D. N. 22n14, 35n7, 53n13, 128n4
Stokes, A. 35n10
subjective 35, 38, 41, 107
Sugarman, A. 34n6, 109n28
symbiosis 31, 135
symbolization 4, 5, 7, 8, 11, 14, 25, 28, 29, 31, 32, 34, 35, 39, 71, 89, 101, 109, 117, 120, 124, 139–41, 144
symptom 15, 70, 79, 89, 91, 96, 99, 100, 101, 105

Target, M. 9, 11, 13, 73n13
therapy 2, 19, 22, 47, 49, 53, 57, 63, 71, 72, 77, 80, 83, 84, 88, 90, 91, 94, 95, 96, 97, 98, 101, 102, 104, 105, 106, 115, 124, 127, 130, 134; group 82, 86–9, 91, 94, 96, 98, 99, 100, 101, 102, 103, 105, 106, 107, 121, 124, 127; mother and child 49, 112, 115, 127
third: analytic 19, 38, 42, 59, 60, 65, 67, 68, 69, 71, 72, 90, 109, 124
thought: oneiric 3, 100, 105
Tisseron, S. 22n21, 24
Tomasi di Lampedusa, G. 23, 34n1
transference 2, 24, 26, 27, 33, 34, 57, 65
transformation 3, 5, 10, 20, 24, 25, 28, 30, 34, 41, 42, 45, 55, 58, 59, 60, 62, 67–70, 72, 76, 78, 80, 88, 89, 90, 94, 106, 107, 109, 110, 117, 118, 131, 133, 134, 138, 139, 140, 142, 144; *see also* loving; passivity and activity
trauma 2, 83, 151
Tronick, E. Z. 22n14, 53n13
truth 22, 48, 54, 55, 56, 58, 59, 60, 61, 62, 64, 66, 68, 70, 71, 73, 87, 105, 107, 109
Tuch, R. H. 128n6
Tustin, F. 140, 144, 145n2, n12, n13, n15, n20

unconscious 2, 3, 4, 5, 6, 7, 11, 13, 18, 19, 20, 27, 28, 32, 33, 38, 41, 42, 44, 46, 50, 51, 52, 56, 58, 59, 62, 65, 67, 72, 78, 80,

82, 83, 85, 86, 88, 90, 91, 92, 93, 101, 102, 106, 107, 109, 114, 117, 122, 124, 126, 127

Vallino, D. 109n4
Van Buren, J. 145n9
Van Gogh, V. 121
Vermeer, J. 85
violence 12, 43, 44, 65, 115, 119, 121, 123; *see also* aggressiveness

Wallenda, N. 129, 145n1
Wangh, M. 22n6

Watterson 110, 112, 114, 116, 117, 118, 122, 125, 126, 128n1
Weinshel, E. M. 73n17
Weiss, S. 109n6
Wilkinson, S. 73n23
Winnicott, D. W. 5, 6, 22n11, n12, n20, 35n8, 37, 38, 46, 49, 50, 51, 52n5, 53n11, n15, n16, n18, n19, n22, n23, n24, 62, 73n26, n40, 87, 91, 109n8, n9, n17, 128n6, n12, 132, 145n7
Woolf, V. 1, 2, 4, 19, 21n1, 22n3, n24

Zagagnoni, L. 22n7